VOLUME 6

NEW TESTAMENT

THE NEW COLLEGEVILLE BIBLE COMMENTARY

GALATIANS AND ROMANS

Robert J. Karris, O.F.M.

SERIES EDITOR

Daniel Durken, O.S.B.

LITURGICAL PRESS

Collegeville, Minnesota

www.litpress.org

Nihil obstat: Robert C. Harren, *Censor deputatus.*
Imprimatur: ✠ John F. Kinney, Bishop of St. Cloud, Minnesota, August 30, 2005.

Design by Ann Blattner.

Cover illustration: *Tree of Life* carpet page at end of Luke by Sally Mae Joseph. Natural hand-ground ink on calfskin vellum, 15-7/8" X 24-1/2." Copyright 2005 *The Saint John's Bible* and the Hill Museum & Manuscript Library at Saint John's University, United States of America.

Photos: pages 10, 36, 60, David Manahan, O.S.B.; pages 16, 28, 42, Corel Photos; page 82, Liturgical Press Photo.

1   2   3   4   5   6   7   8   9

Library of Congress Cataloging-in-Publication Data

Karris, Robert J.
    Galatians and Romans / Robert J. Karris.
        p. cm. — (The new Collegeville Bible commentary. New Testament ; v. 6)
    Summary: "Complete biblical texts with sound, scholarly based commentary that is written at a pastoral level; the Scripture translation is that of the New American Bible with Revised New Testament and revised Psalms (1991)" —Provided by publisher.
    Includes bibliographical references.
    ISBN-13: 978-0-8146-2865-2 (pbk. : alk. paper)
    ISBN-10: 0-8146-2865-6 (pbk. : alk. paper)
        1. Bible. N.T. Galatians—Commentaries.   2. Bible. N.T. Romans—Commentaries.   I. Title.   II. Series.
BS2685.53.K37 2005
227'.1077—dc22
                                                                                    2005012376

CONTENTS

ABBREVIATIONS

Books of the Bible

Acts—Acts of the Apostles
Amos—Amos
Bar—Baruch
1 Chr—1 Chronicles
2 Chr—2 Chronicles
Col—Colossians
1 Cor—1 Corinthians
2 Cor—2 Corinthians
Dan—Daniel
Deut—Deuteronomy
Eccl (or Qoh)—Ecclesiastes
Eph—Ephesians
Esth—Esther
Exod—Exodus
Ezek—Ezekiel
Ezra—Ezra
Gal—Galatians
Gen—Genesis
Hab—Habakkuk
Hag—Haggai
Heb—Hebrews
Hos—Hosea
Isa—Isaiah
Jas—James
Jdt—Judith
Jer—Jeremiah
Job—Job
Joel—Joel
John—John
1 John—1 John
2 John—2 John
3 John—3 John
Jonah—Jonah
Josh—Joshua
Jude—Jude
Judg—Judges
1 Kgs—1 Kings

2 Kgs—2 Kings
Lam—Lamentations
Lev—Leviticus
Luke—Luke
1 Macc—1 Maccabees
2 Macc—2 Maccabees
Mal—Malachi
Mark—Mark
Matt—Matthew
Mic—Micah
Nah—Nahum
Neh—Nehemiah
Num—Numbers
Obad—Obadiah
1 Pet—1 Peter
2 Pet—2 Peter
Phil—Philippians
Phlm—Philemon
Prov—Proverbs
Ps(s)—Psalms
Rev—Revelation
Rom—Romans
Ruth—Ruth
1 Sam—1 Samuel
2 Sam—2 Samuel
Sir—Sirach
Song—Song of Songs
1 Thess—1 Thessalonians
2 Thess—2 Thessalonians
1 Tim—1 Timothy
2 Tim—2 Timothy
Titus—Titus
Tob—Tobit
Wis—Wisdom
Zech—Zechariah
Zeph—Zephaniah

The Letter to the Galatians

I write this commentary for beginners and those who want a quick re-
fresher course for preaching. But this is not a "commentary for dummies,"
for I envision my beginning readers as people who want clear but not
simplistic exposition. I stand on the shoulders of other commentators and
will acknowledge them, especially the premier commentator of our era,
J. Louis Martyn.

To get us thinking about the complex thought world behind the letter
to the Galatians, I tell the story of the poor friars who planned to raise
money for a new bell tower by selling flowers from the friary garden.
Their business became so popular that it adversely affected the trade of
the local florist, who tried by various means to get the friars to sell honey
or bread instead. Finally, he hired the local thug, Hugh McNails, who beat
up the friars and persuaded them to close their flower shop. The moral of
the story is: Only Hugh can prevent florist friars.

Readers from the United States might groan over the moral of this
story, but they would get the pun. But readers from Europe would have a
hard time understanding what was going on. You see, for some sixty years
the Ad Council, along with the federal and state governments, has been so
successful in promoting a slogan that 95 percent of U.S. adults and 77 percent of children recognize Smokey Bear and his slogan: "Only you can
prevent forest fires." So it is understandable that Americans would recognize the pun.

In reading Galatians, we Americans are often like people from Europe
who have not been exposed to Smokey Bear's slogan. When Paul talks
about "the elemental powers" in Galatians 4:9, people of his time would
know what he is referring to, whereas we scratch our heads in wonder-
ment. The Jews of Paul's day would have little difficulty picking up on
Paul's references to Abraham in Galatians 3–4, whereas Gentiles at that
time and we today might be left in the dark.

Let me take the Smokey Bear slogan a step further. Behind that slogan
stand an entire governmental structure and a view of society. Who has the
power to influence 280 million people to hold such name recognition if

not the federal government, which promotes freedom of speech and which has power across state lines? The appeal to "you," an individual, and not to communities is quintessentially American. In a similar way, behind the phrase "the elemental powers" stands a view of reality in which the four powers of water, air, earth, and fire are the elementary building blocks of the world. Behind the name "Abraham" stands the entire story of God's dealings with the chosen people. In brief, this commentary aims to see what stories are at work in Galatians.

What makes Galatians tick?

Galatians is so short that readers sometimes think that it will be a breeze to read and comprehend. But after Paul's relatively simple narrative account in chapters 1 and 2, readers may stumble through the rest of the letter. Let me isolate the building blocks of Galatians and point to the cement that holds these blocks together.

The master plan of Galatians is that of an R&R letter: rebuke, which commences at 1:6, and request, which begins at 4:12. The most evident building blocks of this master plan are its beginning in 1:1-5 and its conclusion in 6:11-18. As we will see in the commentary proper, astute readers can pretty well discover the main thrust of Galatians from these two blocks of material. Paul tells the Galatians what he wants to say, then says his piece, and summarizes what he has said.

The largest building blocks are twofold: situational and preformed. What I call the preformed materials comprise the vast majority of Galatians: Paul's apologetic autobiography in 1:11–2:21, his argument from Scripture in 3:5–4:7, his scriptural allegory in 4:21-31, and his exhortations in 5:1–6:10. While these materials are not exactly cookie-cutter pieces, they give the impression that Paul has used them before. On the other hand, the situational building blocks are the means by which Paul makes Galatians and its preformed materials distinct, much as exterior and interior designs make "seen-one-seen-them-all" houses distinct in large subdivisions. Also, it is from these situational sections that we glimpse what is going on behind the scenes in Galatians 1:1-5; 1:6-10; 3:1-5; 4:8-11; 4:12-20; 5:2-12; 6:11-18.

The cement that holds these building blocks together consists of the three components of Paul's rhetoric. Like any good speaker or writer, Paul has to establish or reinforce his position as a person of trust, integrity, and goodwill. The Greeks called this *ethos,* from which our word "ethics" derives. Paul consumes almost all of Galatians 1–2 reestablishing his trustworthiness: his gospel is from God, not from human beings.

As a good speaker, Paul argues his case according to the *logic* of the time. He uses the argument of examples. He himself and Abraham are examples in Galatians 1–3. Paul also argues from accepted principles of faith. I give two examples. In 5:1 Paul first states the premise and then draws the conclusion, introducing it with the inferential adverb "so" (*oun* in Greek): "For freedom Christ set us free; *so* stand firm and do not submit again to the yoke of slavery." Sometimes Paul states his conclusion first and then enunciates his premise. A good example occurs in 5:4-6. In 5:4 Paul gives his conclusion from the two principles of faith he first articulates in 5:5-6. I put in italics the inferential particle "for" (*gar* in Greek):

> 5:4. You are separated from Christ, you who are trying to be justified by law; you have fallen from grace. 5. *For* through the Spirit, by faith, we await the hope of righteousness. 6. *For* in Christ Jesus, neither circumcision nor uncircumcision counts for anything, but only faith working through love.

Finally, Paul uses *pathos* to engage the hearts of his listeners. I give two quick examples. Who can read Galatians 4:13-20 and not realize that Paul is smuggling himself into the hearts of his beloved Galatian brothers and sisters: "So now have I become your enemy by telling you the truth?" (4:16). Galatians 1:6 is a wake-up slap in the face: "I am amazed that you are so quickly forsaking the one who called you!!" I recall in this context a cartoon that shows Paul with a startled look on his face as he reads a letter: "You have time to write to the Corinthians, the Thessalonians, the Philippians, but I'm amazed that you're too busy to sit down and write a simple letter to your mother!"

These three ingredients of Paul's rhetoric are operative today. Analyze any president's State of the Union address, and you'll see ethos, logic, and pathos on dress parade. This example also prepares us for reading Galatians, for not everyone on both sides of the aisle will be giving a standing ovation for every argument the president makes. Did all Galatians applaud Paul's letter to them? Were the teachers/influencers won over by Paul's argumentation?

The teachers or influencers from outside

I agree with contemporary scholars who avoid the labels "Judaizers" or "opponents" to talk about the people behind the scenes who occasioned Galatians. I will follow J. Louis Martyn and Mark D. Nanos, who call these outsiders "the teachers" and "the influencers" respectively. The scholarly community mainly uses the method of mirror reading to ascertain what these teachers/influencers were advocating. That is, scholars accentuate the situational building blocks and from them try to discern why Paul is using the preformed materials he selects. Finally, they reconstruct through these mirrors what was happening in the Galatian churches.

For example, in the situational materials on Galatians 1:1-5, Paul underscores his call to be an apostle from Jesus Christ and not from human beings. So the inference is made that the teachers/influencers were saying that the gospel Paul preaches to the Gentiles is of human origin. The preformed materials of Galatians 1–2 seem to corroborate that inference, for Paul argues mightily that his gospel came from divine revelation and not from the earlier apostles, who, indeed, did not force him to alter his gospel.

Another example occurs in Galatians 3:1-5, where Paul argues that the Galatians' faith came from Paul's preaching and the Spirit and not from works of the law (including circumcision). The remainder of chapter 3 will deal with the case of Abraham, to whom the promise was made before the mandate of circumcision. In brief, we infer from these indications that the teachers/influencers asserted that the Galatian Christian males had to be circumcised and that all Galatian Christians had to observe the Jewish law to be true Christians.

Date and destination

I date Galatians between A.D. 50 and 55, and thus before Romans. I tend to agree with J. Louis Martyn that Paul wrote it to his converts in North Galatia, or the territory of Galatia, and not to his converts in South Galatia, or the Roman province of Galatia.

The Letter to the Galatians

I. Address

1 **Greeting.** ¹Paul, an apostle not from human beings nor through a human being but through Jesus Christ and God the Father who raised him from the dead, ²and all the brothers who are with me, to the churches of Galatia: ³grace to you and peace from God our Father and the Lord Jesus Christ, ⁴who gave himself for our sins that he might rescue us from the present evil age in accord with the will of our God and Father, ⁵to whom be glory forever and ever. Amen.

ADDRESS

Galatians 1:1-5

1:1-5 Salutation and anticipation of the letter's theme

If you compare this salutation with the salutations of the other genuine Pauline letters, except the letter to the Romans, you will note that Paul has expanded his normal greeting. Take, for example, the salutation in 1 Thessalonians 1:1: "Paul, Silvanus, and Timothy to the church of the Thessalonians in God the Father and the Lord Jesus Christ: grace to you and peace." Galatians 1:1-5 retains the skeleton of the typical Pauline greeting: "Paul to . . ., grace to you and peace," but has much more.

Galatians 1:1 makes two key points. First, Paul underlines the fact that he is the one sent, the apostle of Jesus Christ and God the Father, and not the emissary of some human being, no matter how exalted. Paul will focus on this factor in even greater detail in 1:11–2:21. The second point that Paul makes in Galatians 1:1 is that God the Father raised Jesus from the dead. What had been expected to occur at the end of time in Jewish eschatological expectation, namely, the resurrection of the dead, has broken into time and space now in the resurrection of the Jewish Messiah, Christ Jesus. In the light of this event, can business in the Jewish and Christian communities be conducted as usual?

▶ This symbol indicates a cross reference number in the *Catechism of the Catholic Church*. See page 105 for number citations.

II. Loyalty to the Gospel

⁶I am amazed that you are so quickly forsaking the one who called you by [the] grace [of Christ] for a different gospel ⁷[not that there is another]. But there are some who are disturbing you and wish to pervert the gospel of Christ. ⁸But even if we or an angel from heaven should preach [to you] a gospel other than the one that we preached to you, let that one be accursed! ⁹As we have said before, and now I say again, if anyone preaches to you a gospel other than the one that you received, let that one be accursed!

¹⁰Am I now currying favor with

The second notable expansion of Paul's normal greeting is found in Galatians 1:4, where he probably quotes an early confession that uses sacrificial terminology and then modifies it with one that employs apocalyptic terms. The confession reads: The Lord Jesus has given himself to take away our sins, that is, to eliminate the death-bearing effects of our sins. Implied is the fact that Jesus the Lord did this through the sacrifice of himself on the cross and not through obedience to the law. Using apocalyptic expressions, Paul states that the result and purpose of Jesus' death are our rescue from the present evil age.

Further, Jesus' death has end-of-the-world implications, for it has rescued believers, both Gentiles and Jews, from the present evil age, where sin and death roam about and take captive for their purposes even such a good thing as the law, God's gift to Israel. In brief, Paul anticipates his theme. With the death and resurrection of Jesus, the end of time has come forward and the new creation has begun (see Gal 6:15).

LOYALTY TO THE GOSPEL

Galatians 1:6-10

1:6-10 The beginning of the rebuke part of Galatians

While other letters in antiquity and Paul's letters follow the greeting with a thanksgiving period, Galatians does not. Was Paul so angry with the Galatians that he shot right past the normal courtesy of a thanksgiving? No, he adapted the rebuke statement that was also common in letter writing after the greeting. I paraphrase a pertinent example: "I am amazed that after all my instruction, you have botched the job, etc." The rebuke presupposes some close relationship between the sender and the recipient of the letter. Paul will be spelling out the reasons for his rebuke right up to 4:12, where he makes his request.

In Galatians 1:6 Paul makes it very clear that some of the Galatians are in the process, not of forsaking him and his preaching, but of forsaking God and the new creation they are enjoying. In the situational verse, Galatians

An arched aqueduct in Antioch in Pisidia, a city in central Asia Minor evangelized by Paul and Barnabas

human beings or God? Or am I seeking to please people? If I were still trying to please people, I would not be a slave of Christ.

III. Paul's Defense of His Gospel and His Authority

His Call by Christ. [11]Now I want you to know, brothers, that the gospel preached by me is not of human origin. [12]For I did not receive it from a human being, nor was I taught it, but it came through a revelation of Jesus Christ.

[13]For you heard of my former way of life in Judaism, how I persecuted the church of God beyond measure and tried to destroy it, [14]and progressed in Judaism beyond many of my contemporaries among my race, since I was even more a zealot for my ancestral traditions. [15]But when [God], who from my mother's womb had set me apart and called me through his grace, was pleased [16]to reveal his Son to me, so that I might proclaim him to the Gentiles, I did not immediately consult flesh and blood, [17]nor did I go up to Jerusalem to

1:7, he also provides another hint of what is happening among the Galatians, for "some . . . are disturbing" them. The "disturbance" in question is not a telemarketer calling at dinnertime or someone playing loud music at two in the morning. Rather the disturbance is moral, on the level of conscience.

I find a wonderful parallel in 1 Thessalonians 1:9-10, where Paul reminds his Gentile converts that they "turned to God from idols to serve the living and true God and to await his Son from heaven, whom he raised from [the] dead, Jesus, who *delivers us from the coming wrath*" (emphasis added). It seems that the teachers/influencers are telling the Galatians that Paul's gospel will not deliver them from God's wrath. In our terms, unless the Galatians supplement Paul's teaching with theirs, they're going to hell.

PAUL'S DEFENSE OF HIS GOSPEL AND HIS AUTHORITY
Galatians 1:11–2:21

1:11-24 Paul, zealot for ancestral traditions, becomes apostle to Gentiles

Among the major points in Galatians 1:11–2:21 is Paul's example. Paul insists: Even though I was a zealot for Judaism and its ancestral traditions, I gave it all up. Thus this section prepares for Paul's plea in 4:12: "Be as I am, because I have also become as you are." Paul is saying: "You Galatians are trying to go back to where I was before Christ's revelation of a new creation to me. Don't do it." Parallels to Paul's call are best found in Philippians 3:4-16, where Paul accentuates his zeal for observance of the law: "In righteousness based on the law I was blameless" (Phil 3:6).

those who were apostles before me; rather, I went into Arabia and then returned to Damascus.

¹⁸Then after three years I went up to Jerusalem to confer with Cephas and remained with him for fifteen days. ◄ ¹⁹But I did not see any other of the apostles, only James the brother of the ◄ Lord. ²⁰(As to what I am writing to you, behold, before God, I am not lying.) ²¹Then I went into the regions of Syria and Cilicia. ²²And I was unknown personally to the churches of Judea that are in Christ; ²³they only kept hearing that "the one who once was persecuting us is now preaching the faith he once tried to destroy." ²⁴So they glorified God because of me.

2 The Council of Jerusalem. ¹Then after fourteen years I again went up to Jerusalem with Barnabas, taking Titus along also. ²I went up in accord with a revelation, and I presented to them the gospel that I preach to the Gentiles— but privately to those of repute—so that I might not be running, or have run, in vain. ³Moreover, not even Titus, who was with me, although he was a Greek, was compelled to be circumcised, ⁴but because of the false brothers secretly brought in, who slipped in to spy on our freedom that we have in Christ Jesus, that they might enslave us—⁵to them we did not submit even for a moment, so that the truth of the gospel might remain intact for you.

Another major point in this section is Paul's insistence that his gospel for and to the Gentiles did not come to him from human agency or human tradition, even that of Cephas (Peter), but from revelation. It was God who called Paul as God earlier had called prophets such as Jeremiah and revealed his Son to Paul (1:15-16). From Galatians 1:4 we know that the word "Son" is shorthand for the Son's significance in the story of humankind: The Son, who died for our sins and was raised from the dead, rescues Jews and Gentiles from this evil age.

2:1-14 Paul fights for inclusive table fellowship

As Paul continues his apology for his apostolic ministry and gospel to the Gentiles, we should keep in mind the wise counsel of George Lyons: "Ancient autobiographies were more concerned with ethical characterization and edification than with chronology and exactitude" (p. 60). So Luke's account in Acts 15 and Paul's account here of what happened at the Council of Jerusalem may both be true, since they are told from two different perspectives.

Paul's main points are threefold. The first point concerns the rite of circumcision, by which males entered into the chosen people and committed themselves to observe God's gift of the law. The leaders of the Jerusalem church did not compel Paul to circumcise Titus (2:3) or add the ritual of circumcision to his apostolic ministry (2:6).

⁶But from those who were reputed to be important (what they once were makes no difference to me; God shows no partiality)—those of repute made me add nothing. ⁷On the contrary, when they saw that I had been entrusted with the gospel to the uncircumcised, just as Peter to the circumcised, ⁸for the one who worked in Peter for an apostolate to the circumcised worked also in me for the Gentiles, ⁹and when they recognized the grace bestowed upon me, James and Cephas and John, who were reputed to be pillars, gave me and Barnabas their right hands in partnership, that we should go to the Gentiles and they to the circumcised. ¹⁰Only, we were to be mindful of the poor, which is the very thing I was eager to do.

Peter's Inconsistency at Antioch. ¹¹And when Cephas came to Antioch, I opposed him to his face because he

The second point occurs twice, in 2:5 and 2:14: "the truth of the gospel." While the good news or gospel at Paul's time might refer to a military victory or the birth of an emperor who would change the world and effect lasting peace, for Paul the gospel of Jesus Christ has the power to save through the gift of the Spirit and effects a new creation amidst the old structures of the world. The new creation effected by the gospel has replaced any distinction based on circumcision and uncircumcision: "For neither does circumcision mean anything, nor does uncircumcision, but only a new creation" (Gal 6:15). This is the truth of the gospel; this is "our freedom that we have in Christ Jesus" (2:4). In Paul's view, the teachers/influencers want to liberate the Galatians from this freedom and enslave them by means of circumcision and observance of the law (2:4).

A question introduces the third point: Why the big fuss over who eats what with whom? I answer that food and drink are languages. Do you eat hot dogs on Christmas? Do you toast the bride and groom with water at a wedding? Indeed, not all days are equal; some should be celebrated with better-quality food and drink. Religion also enters into the area of food and drink, as Christians quickly realize when they reflect on the eucharistic bread and wine and Roman Catholics recall their obligation to fast and abstain on Good Friday.

As is the case today, during Paul's time the quality and quantity of food and drink were also social markers. Even at the same symposium, which consisted of eating, a libation to the gods, and drinking with conversation, the patron may have received better food, while his clients were given inferior fare. Jews may have sat in the same room with Gentiles but dined at their own table on specially prepared kosher food and drink. It seems to me that Philip Esler has provided a very helpful way to view what was happening during table fellowship in Antioch. As Jewish

clearly was wrong. ¹²For, until some people came from James, he used to eat with the Gentiles; but when they came, he began to draw back and separated himself, because he was afraid of the circumcised. ¹³And the rest of the Jews [also] acted hypocritically along with him, with the result that even Barnabas was carried away by their hypocrisy. ¹⁴But when I saw that they were not on the right road in line with the truth of the gospel, I said to Cephas in front of all, "If you, though a Jew, are living like a Gentile and not like a Jew, how can you compel the Gentiles to live like Jews?"

Faith and Works. ¹⁵We, who are Jews by nature and not sinners from among the Gentiles, ¹⁶[yet] who know that a person is not justified by works of the law but through faith in Jesus Christ, even we have believed in Christ Jesus that we may be justified by faith in Christ and not by works of the law, because by works of the law no one will be justified. ¹⁷But if, in seeking to be justified in Christ, we ourselves are found to be sinners, is Christ then a minister of sin? Of course not! ¹⁸But if I am building up again those things that I tore down, then I show myself to be a transgressor. ¹⁹For through the law I died

and Gentile Christians shared one loaf and one cup, some Jewish Christians were overwhelmed with the fear that a Gentile Christian, not having completely forgotten idolatrous ways, may have secretively offered a drop of eucharistic wine to a god. How could a person put oneself in the position of participating in such idolatry?

2:15-21 Righteousness, the works of the law, and faith

There are three issues in Galatians 2:16. The meaning of righteousness or justification is the first one. The image seems to stem from the criminal law court system, where a person (or a people) is acquitted, vindicated, judged in the right. Helpful background is Psalm 143:1-2:

> LORD, hear my prayer;
>> in your faithfulness listen to my pleading;
>> answer me in your justice.
> Do not enter into judgment with your servant;
>> before you no living being can be just.

When sinful human beings as God's elect appear before God's law court, God in gracious mercy acquits them; they do not justify or acquit themselves. Modern computer technology has come to our interpretive aid in this matter by supplying the example of word-processing programs that justify margins, that is, they make them straight. Without word processing, the words on this page would not have straight left and right margins but would be out of order, in chaos.

to the law, that I might live for God. I have been crucified with Christ; ²⁰yet I live, no longer I, but Christ lives in me; insofar as I now live in the flesh, I live by faith in the Son of God who has loved me and given himself up for me. ²¹I do not nullify the grace of God; for if justi-fication comes through the law, then Christ died for nothing.

IV. Faith and Liberty

3 **Justification by Faith.** ¹O stupid Galatians! Who has bewitched you,

---

The second issue concerns the meaning of "the works of the law." From the immediate context of Galatians 1–2, it seems that the phrase "the works of the law" refers to those things that distinguish Jews from Gentiles, namely, circumcision, dietary laws, and festivals. But from Galatians 3–4 it seems better to take "the works of the law" in a more comprehensive sense to refer to observance of the law.

In the third issue, grammar and christology hold hands: Is the Greek genitive *Iesou Christou* objective, subjective, or authorial? For years scholars have taken it to be objective, that is, "faith in Jesus Christ." A more appealing interpretation is to take this genitive to be subjective, that is, "the faithfulness that Jesus Christ manifested in his death on the cross for us." If the genitive is authorial, then Jesus Christ is the author of both his and the Christians' faith.

From these three considerations I draw some conclusions. Paul is not attacking the Jews as an arrogant people who are trying to earn heaven by their meritorious deeds. Paul gives himself as an example of how a Jewish zealot became the preacher of a law-free gospel to Gentiles. Through Christ's death and resurrection for us, God has shown a new way of being righteous with God's people. Men do not need to be circumcised, people do not need to observe dietary laws and the sabbath to become members of God's people in Christ. As we will soon see in chapter 3, Paul deals with the big picture—the story of how God fashions a community of faith by liberating people from the powers of the old age and inaugurating a new creation.

FAITH AND LIBERTY

Galatians 3:1–4:31

3:1-5 The Spirit's role in Christian life

Galatians 3:1-5 begins another long section of rebuke and personal example. In a culture that cherished wisdom, Paul's rebuke of the foolishness of the Galatians is harsh. The example that follows throughout

The stadium at Miletus, a seaport on the western coast of Asia Minor where Paul met the elders of Ephesus (see Acts 20:15, 17)

before whose eyes Jesus Christ was publicly portrayed as crucified? ²I want to learn only this from you: did you receive the Spirit from works of the law, or from faith in what you heard? ³Are you so stupid? After beginning with the Spirit, are you now ending with the flesh? ⁴Did you experience so many things in vain?—if indeed it was in vain. ⁵Does, then, the one who supplies the Spirit to you and works mighty deeds among you do so from works of the law or from faith in what you heard? ⁶Thus Abraham "believed God, and it was credited to him as righteousness."

⁷Realize then that it is those who have faith who are children of Abraham. ⁸Scripture, which saw in advance that God would justify the Gentiles by faith, foretold the good news to Abraham,

---

chapter 3 is that of Abraham, who was justified without circumcision. Galatians 3:1-5, along with 3:6-29, allows us to glimpse the preaching of the teachers/influencers, who are championing "the works of the law," especially circumcision. Paul reminds the Galatians that in a very graphic way he had preached Jesus Christ crucified to them and that they listened to this message, which elicited faith. Their faith did not come from "the works of the law," about which they had not yet heard. The gifts of God's powerful Spirit did not come to them from their performance of "the works of the law," about which they were blissfully ignorant.

Paul draws the logical conclusion from his argument based on the Galatians' actual experience: Are you so stupid that you don't recognize that you have already received God's eschatological gift of the Spirit and don't need to complete your faith or membership in God's people with "the works of the law"? With a telling play on two meanings of the word "flesh," that is, flesh as circumcision of the foreskin and flesh as the realm of human weakness, Paul further castigates the Galatians for their stupidity of beginning in the ways of God's powerful Spirit and ending with the flesh. In 5:13–6:10 Paul will return to this contrast of flesh and Spirit when he gives guidance about Christian conduct.

3:6-29 The story of Abraham, the law, Abraham's seed, and us

There are many starting points for the story of St. Francis of Assisi. Some authors start with Christ's command to Francis: "Repair my house." Others commence with Francis's overcoming of his dread of lepers, pariahs of his society. Still others underscore Francis's profound experience of God, who to Francis was "My God and my All." The stories told from these starting points will have many things in common, for example, the economic situation of the time, the importance of Lateran Council IV, the crusades against another pariah of that society, the Muslim. Each story,

saying, "Through you shall all the nations be blessed." [9]Consequently, those who have faith are blessed along with Abraham who had faith. [10]For all who depend on works of the law are under a curse; for it is written, "Cursed be everyone who does not persevere in doing all the things written in the book of the law." [11]And that no one is justified before God by the law is clear, for "the one who is righteous by faith will live." [12]But the law does not depend on faith; rather, "the one who does these things will live by them." [13]Christ ransomed us from the curse of the law by becoming a curse for us, for it is written, "Cursed be everyone who hangs on a tree," [14]that the blessing of Abraham might be extended to the Gentiles through Christ Jesus, so that we might receive the promise of the Spirit through faith.

---

however, will end up with its singular view of Francis of Assisi and what his life meant then and might mean now.

In 3:6-29 Paul is telling the story of Abraham, the law, Abraham's Seed, which is Christ Jesus, and us. His telling of this story seems very different from the way the teachers/influencers were telling it. Yet both they and Paul were using the same common materials, that is, Israel's Scriptures in their Greek version, the Septuagint. Whereas Paul's starting point is Christ Jesus and his faithfulness, the starting point of the teachers/influencers seems to have been God's covenant made with Abraham, which was sealed by circumcision and in which believers remained by faithfully observing the law.

Notice how often Paul refers in this passage to Jesus Christ, who is Paul's real starting point and the goal of the story of Abraham. See, for example, Galatians 3:16, where Paul interprets God's promise to Abraham and his seed to refer to Christ. Galatians 3:23-29 is permeated with references to Christ Jesus. For example, 3:23 reads: "Before faith came, we were held in custody under law, confined for the faith that was to be revealed." As Sam K. Williams says so well, the word "faith" here is best translated as "Jesus-Christ-faith."

From his starting point of Jesus Christ, Paul returns to the story of Abraham. It seems that the teachers/influencers commenced their story with Genesis 17:10-11, where God instructs Abraham: "And this is the covenant that you shall keep between me and you and your seed after you for their generations. Every male among you will be circumcised . . . this circumcision will be a sign of the covenant between me and you" (author's translation). Paul, however, commences his story of Abraham by quoting Genesis 15:6: "Abraham believed God, and it was credited to him as righteousness" (3:6; author's translation). By selecting Genesis 15:6

19

The Law Did Not Nullify the Promise. ¹⁵Brothers, in human terms I say that no one can annul or amend even a human will once ratified. ¹⁶Now the promises were made to Abraham and to his descendant. It does not say, "And to descendants," as referring to many, but as referring to one, "And to your descendant," who is Christ. ¹⁷This is what I mean: the law, which came four hundred and thirty years afterward, does not annul a covenant previously ratified by God, so as to cancel the promise. ¹⁸For if the inheritance comes from the law, it is no longer from a promise; but God bestowed it on Abraham through a promise.

¹⁹Why, then, the law? It was added for transgressions, until the descendant came to whom the promise had been

---

as his key text, Paul scores the big point that Abraham is the father of faith, not of circumcision, for he believed and was declared righteous before he or his descendant was even circumcised.

Having made his point that God justified Abraham by faith, Paul then turns back to the promise God made to Abraham in Genesis 12:3: "All the nations will be blessed through you" (author's translation). By means of his citations of Genesis 15:6 and 12:3, Paul can conclude against the teachers/influencers: "Consequently, those who have faith [the Gentiles] are blessed along with Abraham who had faith" (Gal 3:9).

In Galatians 3:10-25 Paul uses Scripture and human analogies to deal with the role of God's gift of the law. In 3:10-14 Paul uses four Scripture texts to attack the teachers'/influencers' reading of Deuteronomy that God's blessings descend upon those who obey the law. Against their reading Paul quotes Deuteronomy 27:26: "Cursed be everyone who does not persevere in doing all the things written in the book of the law" (author's translation). Implied is that no one can fully obey the law and therefore falls under the curse. Paul supports his case in 3:11 by quoting Habakkuk 2:4 about the centrality of faith, not the law: "The one who is righteous by faith will live" (author's translation).

Then, in 3:12 Paul summons the Pentateuch to ground his position, as he cites Leviticus 18:5: "The one who does these things [the matters of the law] will live by them" and not find true life. Finally, in a daring soteriological move Paul returns to Deuteronomy 27:26 to pick up the theme of "cursed be everyone" and to integrate it with another passage in Deuteronomy that speaks of "cursed be everyone": "Cursed be everyone who hangs on a tree" (Deut 21:23; author's translation). Paul then professes his faith: "Christ ransomed us from the curse of the law by becoming a curse for us" (3:13).

made; it was promulgated by angels at the hand of a mediator. [20]Now there is no mediator when only one party is involved, and God is one. [21]Is the law then opposed to the promises [of God]? Of course not! For if a law had been given that could bring life, then righteousness would in reality come from the law. [22]But scripture confined all things under the power of sin, that through faith in Jesus Christ the promise might be given to those who believe.

What Faith Has Brought Us. [23]Before faith came, we were held in custody under law, confined for the faith that was to be revealed. [24]Consequently, the law was our disciplinarian for Christ, that we might be justified by faith. [25]But now that faith has come, we are no longer under a disciplinarian. [26]For

---

In Galatians 3:15-18 Paul builds his argument about the deficiency of the law by using an analogy and Scripture. Paul's analogy of a human will and testament employs the same Greek word behind "covenant" *(diatheke)* and depends upon the legality that no one can annul or amend the will once it has been ratified. Reading the Septuagint of Genesis 13:15, 17:8, 24:7, Paul states that God's promise was to Abraham and to his "descendant" in the singular. Of course, in Paul's eyes that singular descendant is Christ (3:16). Calculating the time between Abraham and the Sinai covenant, Paul makes his case that the law, which came 430 years later (see Exod 12:40), cannot annul God's promises made to Abraham and through him to the Gentiles.

In Galatians 3:19-25 Paul gives two answers to his question: "Why, then, the law?" (3:19). Galatians 3:19-22, especially 3:19, provides the first answer: "It was added for transgressions." The context indicates that the law was added to restrain transgressions. In this sense it was the disciplinarian of which Paul talks in 3:24-25. In 3:19 Paul masks God's action in giving the law: "It was promulgated by angels at the hand of a mediator." As Leviticus 26:46 clearly indicates, the mediator was Moses. The role of the angels in the giving of the law finds a parallel in the Septuagint of Deuteronomy 33:2 at the giving of the law: "the angels were with God at God's right hand" (author's translation). See also Acts 7:53.

In a mini-summary of the points he has been making from verse 10 onward, Paul writes: "For if a law had been given that could bring life, then righteousness would in reality come from the law. But scripture confined all things under the power of sin, that through the faithfulness of Jesus Christ the promise might be given to those who believe" (3:21-22; author's translation). Paul will have more to say about the law in Romans 7:12: "So then the law is holy, and the commandment is holy and righteous and good."

through faith you are all children of God in Christ Jesus. ²⁷For all of you who were baptized into Christ have clothed yourselves with Christ. ²⁸There is neither Jew nor Greek, there is neither slave nor free person, there is not male and female; for you are all one in Christ Jesus. ²⁹And if you belong to Christ, then you are Abraham's descendant, heirs according to the promise.

God's Free Children in Christ. ¹I mean that as long as the heir is not of age, he is no different from a slave, although he is the owner of everything, ²but he is under the supervision of guardians and administrators until the date set by his father. ³In the same way we also, when we were not of age, were enslaved to the elemental powers of the world. ⁴But when the fullness of time

In Galatians 3:23-25 Paul gives a second answer to the question "Why the law?" He uses two images: imprisonment (confined in custody) and that of a disciplinarian. Both of these images are severe but point to a temporary reality, until Jesus-Christ-faith has come onto the scene.

Paul concludes his argument with the teachers/influencers by calling the Galatians' attention to baptism, by which they become one in Christ Jesus, who is Abraham's descendant. Galatians 3:28 is most likely a liturgical formula that describes the new eschatological reality of Christian community effected by Christ's death and resurrection and the gift of the promised Spirit. For Paul's purposes, the first line is most important: "There is neither Jew nor Greek"/Gentile. Christian communities are still wrestling with the implementation of the vision of this confessional statement of the new reality in Christ Jesus: "There is neither slave nor free person, there is not male and female; for you are all one in Christ Jesus."

If we go back to my opening example of stories about Francis of Assisi, I would say that one major criterion by which we can judge the truth of each story is this: Does it give life? Using this criterion, I would have to say that Paul's story is true, because it has already given life to the Galatians, who had received the Spirit through Paul's preaching of this story as gospel. The question remains: Will the Galatians reaffirm Paul's story or accept that of the teachers/influencers?

4:1-11 Elemental powers of the world, heirs, and the Spirit's cry of "Abba, Father"

I treat three points. While Galatians 3:23-29 and 4:1-11 repeat certain themes, for example, both refer to baptism (3:27-28; 4:4-8), what is surely different between them is Paul's reference to "the elemental powers of the world" (4:3; see 4:9). In my Introduction (pp. 5–6) I mentioned that when we are faced with this type of jargon, we are like foreigners coming to the

had come, God sent his Son, born of a woman, born under the law, [5]to ransom those under the law, so that we might receive adoption. [6]As proof that you are children, God sent the spirit of his Son into our hearts, crying out, "Abba, Father!" [7]So you are no longer a slave but a child, and if a child then also an heir, through God.

Do Not Throw This Freedom Away. [8]At a time when you did not know God, you became slaves to things that by nature are not gods; [9]but now that you have come to know God, or rather to be known by God, how can you turn back again to the weak and destitute elemental powers? Do you want to be slaves to them all over again? [10]You are

---

United States and trying to figure out the meaning of the pun "Only Hugh can prevent florist friars." I provide the following three parallels. Wisdom 13:1-5 is invective against people who worship the four elements of fire, water, earth, and air and do not infer from these good things the God who made them. Wisdom 13:1 states: "For all people . . . were in ignorance of God, and who from the good things seen did not succeed in coming to the knowledge of the one who is" (author's translation).

In their stories of Abraham, both Philo of Alexandria and Josephus, contemporaries of Paul, depict Abraham as overcoming the pagan worship of the elements as gods and coming to the worship of the true God. In Book I.155–156 of his *Jewish Antiquities,* Josephus writes:

> Abraham determined to renew and to change the opinion all people had then concerning God. For he was the first . . . to publish . . . that there was but one God, the Creator of the universe. . . . . This opinion was derived from the irregular phenomena that were visible both at land and sea, as well as those that happen to the sun, and moon, and all the heavenly bodies (modified translation of William Whiston).

With the above background in mind, we begin to glimpse what was going on behind the scenes in Galatia. The teachers/influencers congratulated the Galatians on giving up their worship of the elements and the festivals associated with their worship and invited them to imitate Abraham, who explored the heavenly bodies to ascertain "days, months, seasons, and years" (4:10). What Abraham discovered is contained now in the Jewish sacred times. Paul's attack on the teachers/influencers and the Galatians is radically christocentric. As he says in 4:3: "In the same way we [Paul the Jew included] also, when we were not of age [and before God sent his Son], were enslaved to the elemental powers of the world." If the Galatians return to observing sacred days, after having received Paul's

observing days, months, seasons, and years. [11]I am afraid on your account that perhaps I have labored for you in vain.

Appeal to Former Loyalty. [12]I implore you, brothers, be as I am, because I have also become as you are. You did me no wrong; [13]you know that it was because of a physical illness that I originally preached the gospel to you, [14]and you did not show disdain or contempt because of the trial caused you by my physical condition, but rather you received me as an angel of God, as Christ Jesus. [15]Where now is that blessedness of yours? Indeed, I can testify to you that, if it had been possible, you would have torn out your eyes and given them to me. [16]So now have I become your enemy by telling you the truth? [17]They show interest in you, but not in a good way; they want to isolate you, so that

---

law-free gospel, they are turning back again to "the weak and destitute elemental powers" (4:9).

The figure of Abraham, the first Gentile believer, is one link between Galatians 4:1-11 and 3:6-29. Another is "heir" (Gal 3:29 and 4:1-2). The law's time to be guardian is over, for God has sent God's Son, born as a human being, born as a Jew, to ransom those under the law, so that both Jews and Gentiles might receive full legal rights as heirs (4:5).

Galatians 4:6 is vitally important: "As proof that you are sons, God sent the Spirit of God's Son into our hearts, crying out, 'Abba, Father'" (author's translation). Here Paul is using the same argument he used so powerfully in 3:1-5: the experience of the Galatians. Paul seems to be making another point by his interchange of pronouns "*you* are sons" and "into *our* hearts." Both Gentile Christians and Jewish Christians (Paul included) are heirs together. Both have the same Father, whose name is given in both Aramaic ("Abba") and Greek.

It is fitting that Paul concludes the "rebuke" part of his letter with a sarcastic rebuke: "Do you want to be slaves to them [the elemental powers] all over again?" (4:9). Paul now turns to his "request."

4:12-20 Paul begins his request and appeals to the affections of his friends

G. Walter Hansen and Richard N. Longenecker make a good case that Paul commences the request section of his letter with Galatians 4:12, which contains the first imperative of the entire letter. Hansen notes that a rebuke letter often concluded with a request for renewal of friendship and a change of conduct. These components are obvious in the short papyrus letter contemporaneous with Paul. I adapt Hansen's text:

you may show interest in them. ¹⁸Now it is good to be shown interest for good reason at all times, and not only when I am with you. ¹⁹My children, for whom I am again in labor until Christ be formed in you! ²⁰I would like to be with you now and to change my tone, for I am perplexed because of you.

> I am amazed (rebuke; see Gal 1:6) that you did not see your way to let me have what I asked you to send by Corbolon, esp. when I desired it for a festival. I beg you (request) to buy (imperative) me a silver seal and to send (imperative) it to me posthaste.

In the midst of expending much energy on showing his integrity (*ethos*) and arguing from Scripture and from the Galatians' experience (logic), Paul now wears his emotions on his sleeve (*pathos*). He is tender as he addresses his converts as "brothers and sisters" (4:12) and "my children" (4:19). Like the good wisdom and evangelical teacher that he is, Paul's first exhortation is: "Be as I am" (4:12). In other words, Paul is not telling the Galatians to do something that he doesn't do himself. In the context of this letter, the focus of this appeal is on Paul's self-sacrificing relinquishment of Jewish conduct that separated Jews from Gentiles (circumcision, dietary laws, sabbath) and his adaptation of Gentile ways.

Paul further appeals to the generous and gracious acceptance he received from the Galatians when he appeared on their doorsteps with a weakness of the flesh. Might this weakness of the flesh be the wounds Paul received for preaching the gospel? See 2 Corinthians 11:24-25: "Five times at the hands of the Jews I received forty lashes minus one. Three times I was beaten with rods, once I was stoned." The Galatians did not spit on Paul and reject him, but would have spent an arm and a leg to assist him.

Galatians 4:17 provides a hazy snapshot of the teachers/influencers: "They show interest in you, but not in a good way; they want to isolate you, so that you may show interest in them." It seems that the teachers/ influencers are courting the Galatians, so that they might separate them from their fellow Gentile Christians and include them in the exclusive club of the Jewish Christians who observe the law. Paul is the champion of inclusivity, not exclusivity. He wants both Jewish and Gentile Christians around the same table.

I recall an experience I had some time ago when I went to a restaurant with an African-American confrere. The owner stopped us near the entrance, looked me in the eye, and addressed me: "This is an exclusive

An Allegory on Christian Freedom. ²¹Tell me, you who want to be under the law, do you not listen to the law? ²²For it is written that Abraham had two sons, one by the slave woman and the other by the freeborn woman. ²³The son of the slave woman was born naturally, the son of the freeborn through a promise. ²⁴Now this is an allegory. These women represent two covenants. One was from Mount Sinai, bearing children for slavery; this is Hagar. ²⁵Hagar represents Sinai, a mountain in Arabia; it corresponds to the present Jerusalem, for she is in slavery along with her children. ²⁶But the Jerusalem above is freeborn, and she is our mother. ²⁷For it is written:

> "Rejoice, you barren one who bore
>   no children;
> break forth and shout, you who
>   were not in labor;

club. You can get a membership card immediately and be seated." I was being courted to leave my confrere behind and enjoy exclusive table fellowship. My confrere and I walked out of the restaurant together and sought an inclusive table. Will the Galatians leave their friend Paul standing at the door as they rush to fill a table in an exclusive club?

4:21-31 You are children of the promise and of the Spirit

There are four keys to unlock the meaning of this troublesome passage. The first key is the supposition that Paul is swept into his interpretation of Sarah, Hagar, and their sons because the teachers/influencers were using these figures to instruct the Galatians to follow the path of Sarah's son, Isaac, whom Abraham circumcised and who inherited the promise. Paul turns the exegetical tables on these teachers/influencers and uses Sarah's son for his purposes of proclaiming that the Gentiles, like Isaac, are heirs of the promise (4:28).

The second key is the meaning of "allegory" (4:24). The Greek verb Paul uses here has the generic meaning "to use analogy or likeness to express something." Like any good preacher, Paul is finding an analogy between the historical events of Genesis 21 and the historical events of his own time. As R.P.C. Hanson says: "He (Paul) is doing what he is doing in his scriptural expositions of I Cor. 9 and 10 and II Cor. 3. . . . He is envisaging a critical situation which took place under the Old Covenant . . . as forecasting and repeated by a situation under the New Covenant" (p. 82).

The third key is the Greek verb that stands behind Galatians 4:25: "It *corresponds*" (emphasis added). Literally the Greek verb *systoichei* means "stands in line with." The reader is to imagine two lines over against each

for more numerous are the children
of the deserted one
than of her who has a husband."

²⁸Now you, brothers, like Isaac, are children of the promise. ²⁹But just as then the child of the flesh persecuted the child of the spirit, it is the same now. ³⁰But what does the scripture say?

"Drive out the slave woman and
her son!
For the son of the slave woman
shall not share the
inheritance with the son"

of the freeborn. ³¹Therefore, brothers, we are children not of the slave woman but of the freeborn woman.

---

other: the troops of General X are arrayed against the troops of General Y. Or the lines may be drawn according to radical contrasts: flesh on one side, Spirit/promise on the other side; slavery on one side, freedom on the opposite side; Hagar on one side, and Sarah on the other. So standing in line with "slave" are Hagar, Ishmael (although never named), flesh, Mount Sinai, the present Jerusalem. Standing in line with "free" are Sarah (although never named), Isaac, promise/Spirit, the Jerusalem above.

The fourth key is Paul's quotation of Isaiah 54:1 in 4:27. As Richard B. Hays says: "Paul's major purpose for citing Isa 54:1 is to evoke Deutero-Isaiah's central theme of God's gracious eschatological restoration of Israel and a universal embrace of the nations" (p. 304). Put briefly, the New Jerusalem, which apocalyptic texts such as Revelation 21 expected at the end of time, has appeared because of the boundary-breaking death and resurrection of Christ Jesus. In it are Gentiles who live without the law.

Now that we have used these four keys to gain entrance to Paul's extended analogy, we are somewhat prepared to appreciate the three conclusions he draws for the Galatian Gentiles. The first is that the Galatians are like Isaac and are children of the promise (4:28). The second depends upon acquaintance with a Targumic tradition that Ishmael harassed Isaac because he was circumcised willingly at age thirteen and therefore was more righteous than Isaac, who was circumcised after a mere eight days (see 4:29). The third is found in the one and only quotation from the law in this passage (see 4:21): "'Drive out the slave woman and her son. / For the son of the slave woman shall not share the inheritance with the son' / of the freeborn." Paul uses Scripture to convince his Galatian converts to do something they should have done at the very beginning: Throw the teachers/influencers out of your community!

V. Exhortation to Christian Living

5 **The Importance of Faith.** [1]For freedom Christ set us free; so stand firm and do not submit again to the yoke of slavery.

[2]It is I, Paul, who am telling you that if you have yourselves circumcised, Christ will be of no benefit to you. [3]Once again I declare to every man who has himself circumcised that he is bound to observe the entire law. [4]You are separated from Christ, you who are trying to be justified by law; you have fallen from grace. [5]For through the Spirit, by faith, we await the hope of righteousness. [6]For in Christ Jesus, neither circumcision nor uncircumcision counts for anything, but only faith working through love.

EXHORTATION TO CHRISTIAN LIVING

Galatians 5:1–6:10

5:1-12 Paul's authoritative appeal that the Galatians stand firm in freedom

Paul's appeals in this section tell us much about Christian freedom, Christian community, and the message of the teachers/influencers. If we go back to my introductory gambit about the slogan "Only you can prevent florist friars (forest fires)," we realize that this makes sense in our American culture of rampant individualism. For the "you" that Smokey Bear is pointing to is an individual, not a community. Paul's view of freedom should be seen from the way Paul uses this term in Galatians. Christians are free to form an inclusive community (3:26-28). They have freedom from the power of sin (3:22), from the power of the law (3:23), from the elemental powers of the world (4:3). As Sam K. Williams says: Christians are free "from the religious and cultural prisons whose darkness breeds prejudice, suspicion, and resentment" (3:26-28).

If the Galatians are circumcised, they will join an exclusive club and be obligated to fulfill all its regulations (5:3). Being circumcised or not being circumcised is no longer a way of joining community, but rather "faith working through love" (5:6). Those who are inspirited by Christ's Spirit through faith manifest Christ's self-sacrificing love for one another in community (see Gal 2:20). If one tries to supplement Christian faith with the ethnic marker of circumcision and tries to be justified by observance of the law, that person has fallen from grace (5:4). "A person is not justified by works of the law but through the faithfulness of Jesus Christ" (2:16; author's translation).

Modern-day stonecutters in Turkey

Be Not Misled. ⁷You were running well; who hindered you from following [the] truth? ⁸That enticement does not come from the one who called you. ⁹A little yeast leavens the whole batch of dough. ¹⁰I am confident of you in the Lord that you will not take a different view, and that the one who is troubling you will bear the condemnation, whoever he may be. ¹¹As for me, brothers, if I am still preaching circumcision, why am I still being persecuted? In that case, the stumbling block of the cross has been abolished. ¹²Would that those who are upsetting you might also castrate themselves!

Freedom for Service. ¹³For you were called for freedom, brothers. But do not use this freedom as an opportunity for the flesh; rather, serve one another

---

From this passage it is very clear that the teachers/influencers were trying to persuade the Galatians to fully join the Christian community by being circumcised (5:2). They are "a little yeast" that is negatively influencing "the whole batch of dough" (5:9). They are causing headaches and heartaches of faith for the Galatians (5:10).

Paul displays angry humor in 5:12. Deuteronomy 23:2 provides the best interpretive parallel: "No one whose testicles have been crushed or whose penis has been cut off, may be admitted into the community of the Lord." Paul says: Those who are cutting off foreskins so that others may gain definitive entry into the community should have their own penises cut off and thus be banned from belonging to the community. Is there any doubt that community is a dominant theme of this passage?

5:13-26 Part One of Paul's ethical appeal:
The apocalyptic battle between Flesh and Spirit

Behind this passage another aspect of Paul's confrontation with the teachers/influencers seems to be raging. These teachers/influencers are saying to the Galatians that once they have been circumcised and become members of the Israel of God, they will have the law to guide them in their moral lives and the community of the law to support them when the evil spirit has led them into sin. To Paul this approach to the ethical life is eschatologically outdated and christologically deficient. I call my readers' attention to Galatians 1:4: The Lord Jesus Christ "gave himself for our sins that he might rescue us from *the present evil age*" (emphasis added). Rescue from the present evil age is not by means of the law but by means of God's Spirit (4:6, 29; 5:16-24). I make three explanatory remarks.

First, J. Louis Martyn is indeed correct to see that Paul is using apocalyptic language here to describe what the results in the moral sphere are of Christ's incursion into "the present evil age." He writes:

through love. [14]For the whole law is fulfilled in one statement, namely, "You shall love your neighbor as yourself." [15]But if you go on biting and devouring one another, beware that you are not consumed by one another.

[16]I say, then: live by the Spirit and you will certainly not gratify the desire of the flesh. [17]For the flesh has desires against the Spirit, and the Spirit against the flesh; these are opposed to each other, so that you may not do what you want. [18]But if you are guided by the Spirit, you are not under the law. [19]Now the works of the flesh are obvious: immorality, impurity, licentiousness, [20]idolatry, sorcery, hatreds, rivalry, jealousy, outbursts of fury, acts of selfishness, dissensions, factions, [21]occasions of envy, drinking bouts, orgies, and the like. I

> The Spirit's war against the Flesh . . . was declared by God when he sent his Son and the Spirit of this Son into the territory of the Flesh. This war is, then, the new-creational struggle, the apocalyptic war of the end-time, the war in which God's forces are the ones on the march. . . ." (pp. 530–531).

Paul's apocalyptic imagery of warfare is clear in Galatians 5:13, for the Greek word behind "opportunity" literally means "a staging area for an army." Galatians 5:17 describes the warfare between flesh and Spirit, which "are opposed to each other." Just as in a real war one's options are curtailed in this war, so that "you may not do what you want." The stakes in this warfare are very high, for "inherit[ance of] the kingdom of God" is the goal and prize. We do a disservice to Paul's thought when we take flesh in either its capitalized or noncapitalized form to refer to sins of the flesh. Flesh is the entire world turned against God; flesh refers to human beings turned in upon themselves and away from God.

Although Paul does not invoke the entire law for moral guidance, he is not antimonian. Through the eschatological experience hoped for in Jeremiah 31:33-34, the Galatians have knowledge of what God wants written on their hearts. As James D. G. Dunn says, they depend "more on inward apprehension of what is the appropriate conduct than on rule book or tradition" (p. 296). Further, "the whole law is fulfilled in one statement, namely, 'You shall love your neighbor as yourself'" (5:14). The Galatian Christians are to be slaves to "one another through love" (5:13), as Paul turns the slave/free dichotomy on its head and says in effect: Sure, you are free, free to be in bondage by love to one another. The first fruit of the Spirit is "love" (5:22). People do not need the law to discern the works of the flesh, for they are "obvious" (5:19). Against the fruit of the Spirit "there is no law" (5:23), as if a generous grocer who is feeding the poor

warn you, as I warned you before, that those who do such things will not inherit the kingdom of God. ²²In contrast, the fruit of the Spirit is love, joy, peace, patience, kindness, generosity, faithfulness, ²³gentleness, self-control. Against such there is no law. ²⁴Now those who belong to Christ [Jesus] have crucified their flesh with its passions and desires. ²⁵If we live in the Spirit, let us also follow the Spirit. ²⁶Let us not be conceited, provoking one another, envious of one another.

6 Life in the Community of Christ. ¹Brothers, even if a person is caught in some transgression, you who are spiritual should correct that one in a gentle spirit, looking to yourself, so that you also may not be tempted. ²Bear one another's burdens, and so you will ful-

---

were responding to her complaining neighbors: "Is there a law against helping the poor?"

Finally, the flesh destroys community. See the "vices" in the middle of the "works of the flesh": "hatreds, rivalry, jealousy, outbursts of fury, acts of selfishness, dissensions, factions, occasions of envy" (5:20-21). See also the anti-community behavior Paul rebukes in Galatians 5:13 and 5:26. But the fruit of the Spirit fosters community: "peace, patience, kindness, generosity, faithfulness, gentleness, self-control" (5:22).

Throughout the centuries Christians have been heirs to the battle Paul is waging in Galatians 5:13-26. One side says: They need detailed laws and regulations to prevent them from sinning. Another side states: They need to be genuinely attentive to the Spirit. For those old enough to remember the immediate post-Vatican II days, I invoke the battles between those who cherished the detailed instructions given in the moral manuals and those who championed works such as Bernard Haring's *The Law of Christ*, which stressed the role of the Spirit in moral life.

6:1-10 Part Two of Paul's ethical appeal: The serious consequences of behavior within the household of faith

I take Galatians 6:10, which Hans Dieter Betz has called the summary and conclusion of Galatians 5:1–6:9, as my starting point. Paul's ethical appeal ends with a universal dimension "do good to all," and with a particular dimension, "especially to those who belong to the family of the faith." This is not a natural family or household, but one formed by faith. In this household there are people who teach and lead their fellow members into a deeper understanding of Christian life (6:6). In it there is fraternal correction, done in a spirit of gentleness and love, as members

fill the law of Christ. [3]For if anyone thinks he is something when he is nothing, he is deluding himself. [4]Each one must examine his own work, and then he will have reason to boast with regard to himself alone, and not with regard to someone else; [5]for each will bear his own load.

[6]One who is being instructed in the word should share all good things with his instructor. [7]Make no mistake: God is not mocked, for a person will reap only what he sows, [8]because the one who sows for his flesh will reap corruption from the flesh, but the one who sows for the spirit will reap eternal life from the spirit. [9]Let us not grow tired of doing good, for in due time we shall reap our harvest, if we do not give up. [10]So then, while we have the opportunity, let us do good to all, but especially to those who belong to the family of the faith.

VI. Conclusion

Final Appeal. [11]See with what large letters I am writing to you in my own hand! [12]It is those who want to make a good appearance in the flesh who are

are socialized into appropriate Spirit-led conduct (6:1). In imitation of Christ's self-sacrificing love manifested in his death on the cross for us (Gal 2:20), members of the faith community bear one another's burdens and thus fulfill the only true law, the law of Christ (6:2).

As a modern example of what Paul is saying, I think of my own religious community of Friars Minor, who are white, African American, Hispanic, and Asian, and who are socialized into what it means to be a community of brothers not so much by rules and regulations, but by the example of fellow friars who have faithfully and creatively followed the guidance of the Spirit.

In Galatians 6:7-9, Paul again reveals the apocalyptic bent of his theology. There are ultimate consequences from deeds sown in the flesh and in the Spirit. But Paul ends his serious reminder with a note of encouragement: "Let us not grow tired of doing good, for in due time we shall reap our harvest, if we do not give up" (6:9).

CONCLUSION

Galatians 6:11-18

6:11-18 Postscript and summary of the letter

As Paul summarizes his message, there are pathos and ethos in his description of himself: I bear in my body the brand marks of Jesus Christ (6:17). Paul's scars are signs of his love for Christ Jesus and the Galatians. Paul continues to attack the teachers/influencers who champion circumcision as the saving supplement to Paul's gospel (6:11-13). In my tradition,

trying to compel you to have your-selves circumcised, only that they may not be persecuted for the cross of Christ. ¹³Not even those having themselves cir-cumcised observe the law themselves; they only want you to be circumcised so that they may boast of your flesh. ¹⁴But may I never boast except in the cross of our Lord Jesus Christ, through which the world has been crucified to me, and I to the world. ¹⁵For neither does circumcision mean anything, nor does uncircumcision, but only a new creation. ¹⁶Peace and mercy be to all who follow this rule and to the Israel of God.

¹⁷From now on, let no one make troubles for me; for I bear the marks of Jesus on my body.

¹⁸The grace of our Lord Jesus Christ be with your spirit, brothers. Amen.

---

it's as if someone were to accost a regular church member and say that he will only be saved if he recites the Novena to St. Anthony of Padua every Tuesday. It is not circumcision that is foundational but the cross. What God has done to Sin and Flesh and Law by the death and resurrection of his Son has changed the world and transformed Paul (6:14).

In Galatians 6:15 Paul introduces the term "new creation." I find a compelling parallel to "new creation" in one of my favorite books from New Testament times. *Joseph and Aseneth* tells the story of the conversion of the Gentile Aseneth so that she could marry Joseph (see Gen 41:45). In Joseph's prayer over Aseneth, I have italicized the "new creation" words: "Lord God of my father Israel, the Most High, the Powerful One of Jacob, who gave life to all things, and called them from darkness to light, and from error to truth, and from death to life, you, Lord, bless this virgin and *renew* her by your spirit, and *form her anew* by your hidden hand, and *make her alive again* by your life" (8.9; modified translation of C. Burchard).

The death and resurrection of the Lord Jesus and the sending of his creative Spirit have brought about the new creation. This new creation, however, is not just revealed in individuals but also and especially in the household of faith, where Jew and Gentile, male and female, slave and freeborn are sitting at the same table, enjoying their freedom in the Spirit, in the midst of the present evil age, and awaiting God's righteousness in hope.

The Letter to the Romans

Dr. Karris recommends a pronoun-rich reading of Romans

How should you approach Romans? Nibble on it piecemeal as the Lectionary does? Or meet it head on? I recommend the courageous second approach. Begin reading chapter 1 and go straight through to chapter 16. Along the way make a detailed list of the personal pronouns Paul uses. How often does he use "I" or "we" or "you" or the third person? Why, for example, does the personal pronoun "we" dominate Romans 5:1-11 and 8:31-39? Who is the "I" of Romans 7:7-25? Why does "I" occur so poignantly and so frequently in Romans 9–11? Who is the "you" of Romans 6:12-23? Why are there so many imperatives in Romans 12:1–15:13?

Further, as you mosey through the text, take a close look at the way Paul begins (1:1-16) and ends (15:14-33) his letter proper and how he insists on his role as the apostle to the Gentiles (1:5, 13; 15:16, 18, 27). In your reading you can't but notice how often Paul buttresses his presentation with quotations from the Greek or Septuagint translation of Scripture, for example, Romans 3:11-17, and you may be envious of the scriptural literacy of the first hearers of his letter.

Be sure not to miss the numerous questions with which Paul energizes his text. For example, Romans 4:1: "What then can we say that Abraham found, our ancestor according to the flesh?" and Romans 11:1: "I ask, then, has God rejected his people? Of course not!" Do you have the feeling that Romans 8:31-39 or Romans 11:33-36 forms a grand conclusion or peroration and are puzzled why Paul soldiers on after these two magnificent confessions of faith?

Although you're tired, struggle through the Roman directory of Romans 16. From a careful reading of 16:1-16, scholars have discerned that there were some five house churches in Rome and that women played a major role in earliest Christianity. If you're not too weary, you may ask why Paul ends his letter with a doxology (16:25-27) rather than a simple wish, as in 1 Corinthians 16:24: "My love to all of you in Christ Jesus." From this courageous and careful hands-on approach you will be in a very good

position to ask and test the answers to such questions as the literary form, addressees, purpose, and messages of Romans.

Check the background you bring to your reading of Romans

Against what background should I read Romans? Various church traditions have provided us with backgrounds. For example, there is the Lutheran background of underscoring human dependence upon God's grace and faith over against legalism in all its forms. Unfortunately, most Roman Catholics bring little informed background to Romans, for Paul's letters, especially Romans, are rarely preached upon during Sunday Mass. Contemporary scholars successfully interpret Romans as a story of God's dealings with humankind going back to Adam, Abraham, the giving of the law, the death and resurrection of the Lord Jesus Christ, and final glory. Others make some good sense of Romans as the gospel of God's love and peace over against the Roman imperial gospel of peace and prosperity.

In this commentary I follow Stanley K. Stowers in reading Romans against the background of the Jewish view of Gentiles. Paul states this Jewish viewpoint very clearly in Galatians 2:15: "We, who are Jews by nature and not sinners from among the Gentiles." This Jewish view of Gentiles is manifest in a passage from the religious romance *Joseph and Aseneth,* which dramatically portrays Joseph's abhorrence of kissing the pagan Aseneth: "It is not fitting for a man who worships God, who will bless with his mouth the living God and eat blessed bread of life . . . to kiss a strange woman who will bless with her mouth dead and dumb idols and eat from their table bread of strangulation and drink from their libation a cup of insidiousness" (8.5-7 in C. Burchard's translation).

The Jewish philosopher Philo of Alexandria champions the view that the law of Moses frees Gentiles from their desires, so that they can achieve their goal of self-mastery over their passions. In Book IV.55 of his *Special Laws,* Philo comments: "The law thinks that all those who adhere to the sacred constitution, established by Moses, ought to be free from all unreasonable passions, and from all wickedness" (C. D. Yonge translation). 4 Maccabees 1:16-19 maintains that wisdom derived from the law is the master of human passions:

> Reason, I suggest, is the mind making a deliberate choice of the life of wisdom. Wisdom, I submit, is knowledge of things divine and human, and of their causes. And this wisdom, I assume, is the culture we acquire from the law, through which we learn the things of God reverently and the things of men to our worldly advantage. The forms of wisdom consist of prudence, justice, courage, and temperance. Of all

37

The Coliseum in Rome hosted public events that included fights between animals, the killing of Christians by lions and other executions, and combats between gladiators.

these prudence is the most authoritative, for it is through it that reason controls the passions (NRSV).

With the above background in mind, we will be able to glimpse how Paul maintains that the Gentile believers' new life in Christ, not works of the law, has given them control over their passions (see 6:12-23). We will better appreciate Paul's indictment of the Gentiles in Romans 1:18-32, his dramatization of the Gentile "I" in 7:7-25, and his exhortations in 12:1–15:13, for example, 12:2: "Do not conform yourself to this age but be transformed by the renewal of your mind, that you may discern what is the will of God, what is good and pleasing and perfect." In brief, we will be better able to understand all of Romans, which reveals the gospel of the Apostle to the Gentiles.

The literary form and purposes of Romans

Scholars have called Romans a letter essay or an ambassadorial letter. I treat Romans as a letter of persuasion, technically a protreptic letter. Its main purpose is to persuade the Gentile Christians in Rome about the truth of Paul's gospel for/to the Gentiles. If they accept Paul's gospel to the Gentiles, they may also be willing to help support Paul's mission to the Gentiles in Spain (15:22-24) with personnel and money.

In writing an account of his gospel to the Gentiles, Paul has one eye on Jerusalem. He is anxious that the saints in Jerusalem accept the money that he has collected from Gentile converts and its symbolism of the unity of his law-free gospel with the gospel preached by Jerusalem. Perhaps this aspect of Paul's purposes accounts for the many quotations from Scripture in Romans, for the Judean Christians could be persuaded by arguments from Sacred Scripture. While it seems clear to me that Paul knew something about the situation in Rome, I am not fully persuaded that a purpose of Romans was to settle the so-called controversy between "the weak" and "the strong" in Romans 14:1–15:13. Why would Paul write the weighty first thirteen chapters of Romans to handle such a relatively small problem? We usually don't eliminate a mosquito with a blunderbuss.

What makes Romans tick?

Those who have taken my earlier recommendation and persevered through a pronoun-rich reading of Romans have gone beyond the spoon-fed selections of Romans from the Sunday Lectionary and are ready for the strong food of rhetorical criticism. The cement that holds the various sections of Romans together is formed from the three ingredients of Paul's rhetoric. Although it is clear that the Roman Christians know who Paul is and that he knows something about them and their circumstances, Paul has to establish his position as a person of integrity, trust, authority, and goodwill, especially in the light of possible slurs about the truth of the gospel he preaches (see Rom 3:7-8). This ingredient of Paul's rhetoric is called *ethos* and is especially prominent in his use of "I" in his introduction to and conclusion of Romans, and I would venture to suggest that Romans 9–11, which uses "I" twenty-seven times, contains much *ethos* (besides considerable *pathos*).

As a superb letter writer, Paul makes his points according to *the logic* of his time. Our preliminary reading has repeatedly discovered one component of Paul's logic, namely, his reliance of the authority of Sacred Scripture. As a matter of fact, it has been calculated that fifty-one of the eighty-nine quotations of Scripture found in Paul's letters occur in Romans, and thirty-nine percent of Romans 9–11 consists of citations from Sacred Writ. Paul normally uses the third person for these quotations.

Sometimes the reason for Paul's use of Scripture is relatively clear to us moderns. For example, the chain of quotations in Romans 3:10-18 refers to the entirety of the thinking, willing, articulate, and acting human being: throats, tongues, lips, mouths, feet, eyes. In Romans 15:9-12 Paul makes his case about the Gentiles by quoting the entirety of Scripture, that is, its three major portions: Law, Prophets, Writings. It goes without saying that Paul expects his hearers to know their Bible.

In our preliminary reading of Romans, we have frequently stumbled across another major component of Paul's logic when we encountered questions such as "What are we to say?" (Rom 4:1; 6:1; 7:7; 8:31; 9:14, 30), or exclamations such as "Of course not" (Rom 3:4, 6, 31; 6:1, 15; 7:7, 13; 9:14; 11:1, 11), or second-person addresses to an imaginary conversation partner, such as Romans 9:19-21:

> You will say to me then: "Why does he still find fault? For who can oppose his will?" But who indeed are you, a human being, to talk back to God? Will what is made say to its maker: "Why have you created me so?" Or does not the potter have a right over the clay, to make out of the same lump one vessel for a noble purpose and another for an ignoble one? (trans. H. Anderson, p. 545; other examples in Rom 2:1-5, 17-29; 8:2; 11:17-24; 14:4, 10).

Technically speaking, this component of Paul's logic bears the name of diatribe, which unfortunately for our understanding has the meaning in contemporary English of "a bitter verbal or written criticism." Stanley

Stowers defines ancient diatribe in this way: "A term for teaching activity in the schools, literary imitations of that activity, or for writings which employ the rhetorical and pedagogical style typical of diatribes in the schools." Typical of the diatribe in the schools were intense dialogues, questions, and answers.

Those familiar with teaching in the Middle Ages recognize a cousin of the diatribe in the "sic et non" and "quaestiones" traditions of the scholastics, as they raised questions and provided answers for and against an interpretation. Contemporary classrooms provide a distant cousin of the diatribe when they feature questions and answers. Finally, it should be noted that the goal of the diatribe modality is pedagogical and hortatory, not polemical, that is, it is motivated by a concern that students learn; it does not arise from Romans' contempt of false opinions. Finally, as Stowers maintains: "It is also a misunderstanding to read dialogical features (e.g., objections) as references to actual groups in the Roman church." I invite advanced students to explore the diatribe style manifested in Epictetus's "Concerning Anxiety" in Book II.13 of his *Discourses.*

Surely the vast majority of us readers are not trained in reading a text that contains a heavy component of the teaching style called diatribe. So we will have to take our time and exercise great patience. To me, this component of Paul's logic shows how carefully he constructed Romans and how he endeavored to engage his hearers and to win them over to full acceptance of his gospel to the Gentiles. Further, just think of how skilled a reader Phoebe was to proclaim Paul's complex letter intelligently and persuasively (Rom 16:1-2) .

Lastly, Paul uses *pathos* to influence the minds of his hearers through engaging their hearts and emotions. Who can miss the *pathos* that floods through Romans 9:1-5; 10:1; 11:1-2; for example, Romans 9:3: "For I could wish that I myself were accursed and separated from Christ for the sake of my brothers, my kin according to the flesh"?

Further, Leander E. Keck has pointed to another dimension of *pathos:* The speaker or author should experience in himself the same emotions he wants to inspire in his hearers. In Book II.47.195 of his *Concerning the Orator,* Cicero writes of how he defended Manius Aquilius in court:

> For here was a man whom I remembered as having been consul, commander-in-chief, honored by the Senate, and mounting in procession to the Capitol. On seeing him cast down, crippled, sorrowing and brought to the risk of all he held dear, *I was myself overcome by compassion before I tried to excite it in others* (Loeb translation modified).

It seems that this characteristic of *pathos* may stand behind Paul's frequent use of "we," for example, in Romans 5:1-11; 7:5-6; 8:31-39, and the exhortatory materials in 12:4; 13:11-12; 14:7-8, 10, 12, 13, 19; 15:1-2, as Paul demonstrates that he shares the same emotions that he wants to evoke in his hearers.

Finally, I invite my readers to take another glance at Romans 15:30-33. Paul is not looking forward to his confrontation with the Judean believers and wants the Romans to join him in the struggle by their prayers on his behalf. In this passage Paul's *ethos* and *pathos* embrace and invite the hearers to storm heaven for his deliverance.

The messages of Romans

In the exposition of individual passages, I will have an opportunity to describe the various messages of Romans. According to my count, there are 146 references to "God" in the sixteen chapters of Romans. This overwhelming number tells me that Romans is about God. In particular, it explains God's actions in the face of apparent injustice. Or as Luke Timothy Johnson says so well: "The argument of Romans is, at root, simple. God is one and God is fair."

A simple outline of Romans

I wholeheartedly encourage my readers to engage in a serious, continuous, and pronoun-rich reading of Romans, and I have composed my commentary to aid such a reading. The following outline presents a basic road map through this long, intricate, and richly rewarding letter that Paul wrote from Corinth about A.D. 57.

Romans 1:1-15 Beginning

Romans 1:16-17 Theme

Romans 1:18–11:36 Body

Romans 12:1–15:13 Exhortations

Romans 15:14-33 Conclusion

Romans 16:1-27 Greetings, a warning, final doxology

The Letter to the Romans

I. Address

1 **Greeting.** ¹Paul, a slave of Christ Jesus, called to be an apostle and set apart for the gospel of God, ²which he promised previously through his prophets in the holy scriptures, ³the gospel about his Son, descended from David according to the flesh, ⁴but established as Son of God in power according to the spirit of holiness through resurrection from the dead, Jesus Christ our Lord. ⁵Through him we have received the grace of apostleship, to bring about the obedience of faith, for the sake of his name, among all the Gentiles, ⁶among whom are you also, who are

---

ADDRESS

Romans 1:1-15

1:1-7 The apostle to the Gentiles introduces himself and his gospel

In these compact verses Paul introduces himself, his gospel, and the gist of his message. He did not take it upon himself to speak for God and God's Son as their apostle. God called him, a zealous persecutor of the church, to be an apostle to the Gentiles (see Gal 1:11-24). I pause here and urge my readers to go back to my Introduction (p. 37) to see what I have to say about the Jewish view of Gentiles: They are sinners. Yet God has called the Jew Paul to preach the gospel to these sinners.

The good news or gospel that Paul preaches is not totally new but has antecedents in the Scriptures (1:2). We will be frustrated if we look exclusively for individual verses in the Old Testament. Paul is looking more to the broad sweep of God's purpose of giving life to women and men. Paul will refer again to God's salvific purpose when he considers Abraham (Rom 4), Adam (Rom 5:12-21), the gift of the law (Rom 7:1–8:30), those powers that try to separate us from God (Rom 8:31-39), and God's election of Israel (Rom 9–11).

The gospel is about God's Son, born a Jew from a royal house, and "established as Son of God in power according to the spirit of holiness through resurrection from the dead, Jesus Christ our Lord" (1:4). Paul

---

▶ This symbol indicates a cross reference number in the *Catechism of the Catholic Church*. See page 105 for number citations.

A view of the Roman Forum with ongoing excavations in the foreground and the Palatine Hill, one of the seven hills of Rome, in the background.

called to belong to Jesus Christ; [7]to all the beloved of God in Rome, called to be holy. Grace to you and peace from God our Father and the Lord Jesus Christ.

Thanksgiving. [8]First, I give thanks to my God through Jesus Christ for all of you, because your faith is heralded throughout the world. [9]God is my witness, whom I serve with my spirit in proclaiming the gospel of his Son, that I remember you constantly, [10]always asking in my prayers that somehow by God's will I may at last find my way clear to come to you. [11]For I long to see you, that I may share with you some

---

makes no mention here that this royal figure was crucified by Roman power. Instead, he uses the eschatological category of resurrection from the dead to indicate that God has done something new and final in Jesus. Death has not conquered Jesus. God has exalted him to be Lord.

Richard A. Horsley has been reminding us that Paul's gospel stands in radical contrast to the imperial gospel, inaugurated by Caesar Augustus, whose victories and rule were considered good news. Augustus was hailed by an inscription at Priene as "[a Savior] who has made war to cease and who shall put everything [in peaceful] order" (F. W. Danker). It is not happenstance that Paul will follow his introduction with an indictment of Gentile idolatry and vices (1:18-32). Jesus, Son of David, Son of God, is Savior and Lord, not Caesar.

It is also significant that Paul exhorts his hearers in Romans 5:1: "Let us have peace with God through our Lord Jesus Christ" (author's translation). Americans who think that emperor worship, bread, and circuses are beyond their ken should take a closer look at American Civil Religion and the United States' multiple shrines dedicated to pleasure, consumerism, and the fountain of youth.

God has called Paul "to bring about the obedience of faith" (1:5). Paul announces here a major theme of Romans, which he will develop at great length with the example of Abraham, who was a Gentile, an ungodly person, but who believed (4:5). Already we hear the briefest of hints about theodicy: Should we Gentiles believe in a God who seems not to have been faithful to the people God first called? If God were not faithful to them, how can we Gentiles have confidence that God will be faithful to us? See Romans 9–11.

1:8-15 Paul gives thanks and states that he worships God through preaching

My sole comment here is on Romans 1:9: "God is my witness, whom I worship with my spirit in proclaiming the gospel of his Son" (author's

spiritual gift so that you may be strengthened, [12]that is, that you and I may be mutually encouraged by one another's faith, yours and mine. [13]I do not want you to be unaware, brothers, that I often planned to come to you, though I was prevented until now, that I might harvest some fruit among you, too, as among the rest of the Gentiles.

[14]To Greeks and non-Greeks alike, to the wise and the ignorant, I am under obligation; [15]that is why I am eager to preach the gospel also to you in Rome.

II. Humanity Lost without the Gospel

God's Power for Salvation. [16]For I am not ashamed of the gospel. It is the

translation). Paul uses the Greek verb *latreuein,* "to worship." His worship of God is through his missionary activity of proclaiming the gospel of the Lord Jesus, not through emperor worship. In Romans 12:1 Paul tells the Romans how to worship: "I urge you therefore, brothers, by the mercies of God, to offer your bodies as a living sacrifice, holy and pleasing to God, your spiritual worship."

In Romans 15:16 Paul again uses worship terminology to describe his preaching of the gospel: "to be a minister of Christ Jesus to the Gentiles in performing the priestly service of the gospel of God, so that the offering up of the Gentiles may be acceptable, sanctified by the holy Spirit." It does not seem to me that Paul is merely using worship language in a figurative way.

HUMANITY LOST WITHOUT THE GOSPEL

Romans 1:16–3:20

1:16-17 Paul states the theme of his letter

My readers can peruse all thirteen of Paul's letters and not find another instance where Paul announces the theme of his letter as he does here, for Romans alone is modeled after a scholastic diatribe or instruction (see Introduction, pp. 39–40). Paul will explicate this theme in the rest of Romans, often by using the questions of scholastic diatribe. While the gospel is God's power for the salvation of all people, it is meant first for God's elect people.

I borrow from two renowned commentators to define "God's righteousness." Joseph A. Fitzmyer accentuates it as an attribute of God who is judge for God's people: "It is a quality whereby God actively acquits his sinful people, manifesting towards them his power and gracious activity in a just judgment. . . ." Ernst Käsemann underscores God's dominion

power of God for the salvation of everyone who believes: for Jew first, and then Greek. [17]For in it is revealed the righteousness of God from faith to faith; as it is written, "The one who is righteous by faith will live."

Punishment of Idolators. [18]The wrath of God is indeed being revealed from heaven against every impiety and wickedness of those who suppress the truth by their wickedness. [19]For what can be known about God is evident to them, because God made it evident to them. [20]Ever since the creation of the world, his invisible attributes of eternal power and divinity have been able to be understood and perceived in what he has made. As a result, they have no excuse; [21]for although they knew God they did not accord him glory as God or give him thanks. Instead, they became vain in their reasoning, and their senseless minds were darkened. [22]While claiming to be wise, they became fools [23]and exchanged the glory of the immortal God for the likeness of an image

over the world: "God's sovereignty over the world revealing itself eschatologically in Jesus . . . the rightful power with which God makes his cause to triumph in the world which has fallen away from him and which yet, as creation, is his inviolable possession."

I believe that we can capture some of the nuances of "from faith to faith" if we look at Paul's quotation from Habakkuk. I translate the Septuagint of Habakkuk 2:4: "The righteous person will live because of my faithfulness." The reference behind "my" is God, who is faithful to the person who has kept right relationship with God. Although Paul has dropped "my," it seems that the background of Habbakuk is still in his mind. The Greek word *pistis,* which is regularly translated by "faith," also means "faithfulness" and "trust." God's righteousness reveals God's faithfulness to God's chosen people and to creation and leads to a faithful response. Would that sermons were preached on the gospel of God's righteous fidelity to God's elect and God's creation!

1:18-32 The plight of the Gentiles

I ask you to skip ahead to Romans 3:21-24. Read that passage carefully: "But now the righteousness of God has been manifested . . . the righteousness of God through faith in Jesus Christ for all who believe. For there is no distinction; all have sinned. . . . They are justified freely by his grace through the redemption in Christ Jesus." It would seem that Romans 3:21-24 is the "logical" next paragraph after Paul's theme sentence in Romans 1:16-17. But before Paul could arrive at this "solution," he had to state the "problem": All have sinned. Put another way, in the style of a scholastic diatribe Paul develops his theme of "God's righteousness unto

of mortal man or of birds or of four-legged animals or of snakes. ²⁴Therefore, God handed them over to impurity through the lusts of their hearts for the mutual degradation of their bodies. ²⁵They exchanged the truth of God for a lie and revered and worshiped the creature rather than the creator, who is blessed forever. Amen. ²⁶Therefore, God handed them over to degrading passions. Their females exchanged natural relations for unnatural, ²⁷and the males likewise gave up natural relations with females and burned with lust for one another. Males did shameful things with males and thus received in their own persons the due penalty for their perversity. ²⁸And since they did not see fit to acknowledge God, God handed them over to their undiscerning mind to do what is improper. ²⁹They are filled with every form of wickedness, evil, greed, and malice; full of envy, murder, rivalry, treachery, and spite. They are gossips ³⁰and scandalmongers and they hate

---

salvation" by contrasting it with its antithesis: sin's domination over humans (see 3:9) and the law's inability to cope with sin (3:20).

The dominant Jewish view of Gentiles pulses through this passage. Later on, in Romans 6:17, Paul will remind his Gentile hearers that they were formerly in the same boat of lacking mastery over self, because they "were once slaves of sin." From the key sin of idolatry all other sins cascade forth. As Wisdom 14:12 states:

> For the source of wantonness is the devising of idols;
>   and their invention was a corruption of life.

And Wisdom 14:25-27 continues:

> And all is confusion—blood and murder, theft and guile,
>   corruption, faithlessness, turmoil, perjury,
> Disturbance of good men, neglect of gratitude,
>   besmirching of souls, unnatural lust,
>   disorder in marriage, adultery and shamelessness.
> For the worship of infamous idols
>   is the reason and source and extremity of all evil.

There is no excuse for such behavior: "For although they knew God they did not accord him glory as God or give him thanks" (1:21; see 1:32).

Contemporary society almost forces us to bypass the capital sins and even murder in Romans 1:29-31 and to focus on what Paul says about same-sex love in 1:24-28. As Richard B. Hays and others have shown, there is no doubt that Paul condemns these actions that are willingly

God. They are insolent, haughty, boastful, ingenious in their wickedness, and rebellious toward their parents. [31]They are senseless, faithless, heartless, ruthless. [32]Although they know the just decree of God that all who practice such things deserve death, they not only do them but give approval to those who practice them.

2 **God's Just Judgment.** [1]Therefore, you are without excuse, every one of you who passes judgment. For by the standard by which you judge another you condemn yourself, since you, the judge, do the very same things. [2]We know that the judgment of God on those who do such things is true. [3]Do you suppose, then, you who judge those who engage in such things and yet do them yourself, that you will escape the judgment of God? [4]Or do you hold his priceless kindness, forbearance, and patience in low esteem, unaware that the kindness of God would lead you to repentance? [5]By your stubbornness and impenitent heart, you are storing up wrath for yourself for the day of wrath and revelation of the just judgment of God, [6]who will repay everyone according to his works: [7]eternal life to those

chosen. Luke Timothy Johnson formulates the question for contemporary application: "Or is it [same-sex love], as some studies and many people claim, the 'natural' mode of sexual expression for a small portion of the world's population?"

2:1-5 The Gentile who boasts

In the very beginning of my Introduction (p. 35), I asked my readers to make their way through all of Romans by asking questions such as: What personal pronouns does Paul use? Romans 2:1-5 is a very important case in point, for Paul changes from the third person pronouns of 1:18-32 to "you" singular. The NAB's translation of Romans 2:1 and 3 masks Paul's use of the Greek *ō anthrōpe,* which is used in scholastic diatribe and means "fellow" or, in our parlance, "guy." I render Romans 2:1, which continues Paul's discussion of how passions rule Gentiles: "Therefore, you are without an excuse, guy, like anyone who judges." Paul's diatribal address picks up "the insolent, haughty, and boastful" Gentiles of Romans 1:30 and skewers them. For they, too, are sinners. Romans 2:4 finds a parallel in Wisdom 11:23:

> But you [God] have mercy on all, because you can do all things;
> and you overlook the sins of men that they may repent.

2:6-16 Three key teachings

Gentiles are still very much in Paul's eyes as he refers to two fundamental beliefs about God that are based in the Scriptures. God "will repay

who seek glory, honor, and immortality through perseverance in good works, [8]but wrath and fury to those who selfishly disobey the truth and obey wickedness. [9]Yes, affliction and distress will come upon every human being who does evil, Jew first and then Greek. [10]But there will be glory, honor, and peace for everyone who does good, Jew first and then Greek. [11]There is no partiality with God.

Judgment by the Interior Law. [12]All who sin outside the law will also perish without reference to it, and all who sin under the law will be judged in accordance with it. [13]For it is not those who hear the law who are just in the sight of God; rather, those who observe the law will be justified. [14]For when the Gentiles who do not have the law by nature observe the prescriptions of the law, they are a law for themselves even though they do not have the law. [15]They show that the demands of the law are written in their hearts, while their conscience also bears witness and their conflicting thoughts accuse or even defend them [16]on the day when, according to my gospel, God will judge people's hidden works through Christ Jesus.

Judgment by the Mosaic Law. [17]Now if you call yourself a Jew and rely on the law and boast of God [18]and know

everyone according to his works" (2:6). Proverbs 24:12 states: God "will repay each one according to his deeds." Romans 2:11 confesses: "There is no partiality with God." Sirach 35:12 professes: "For he is a God of justice, / who knows no favorites." The Gentile is judged by deeds, but so too is the member of God's chosen people, for God is impartial.

A further fundamental belief is imbedded in Romans 2:16: "according to my gospel, God will judge people's hidden works through Christ Jesus." The gospel, for which Paul fought so uncompromisingly in Galatians, is that Gentiles do not have to become Jews and observe the law in order to be justified in God's sight. In turn, Christ Jesus will not judge them on the basis of their observance of Jewish covenantal law but on the observance of the law in their hearts. As Charles H. Talbert comments, "A pervasive belief existed among ancient Jews as well as pagans that all people had some elemental knowledge of morality for which they were responsible."

2:17-29 A pretentious teacher, who is a Jew and would teach Gentiles

Again, note the change of personal pronoun, as third person gives way to "you" singular. Stanley Stowers has helped me to see this passage as a diatribal attack on the pretentious teacher, who happens to be a Jew and is not the "typical Jew." I recall many of J. F. Powers's short stories that featured Roman Catholic clergy. Clergy who read these stories were up in

49

his will and are able to discern what is important since you are instructed from the law, [19]and if you are confident that you are a guide for the blind and a light for those in darkness, [20]that you are a trainer of the foolish and teacher of the simple, because in the law you have the formulation of knowledge and truth—[21]then you who teach another, are you failing to teach yourself? You who preach against stealing, do you steal? [22]You who forbid adultery, do you commit adultery? You who detest idols, do you rob temples? [23]You who boast of the law, do you dishonor God by breaking the law? [24]For, as it is written, "Because of you the name of God is reviled among the Gentiles."

[25]Circumcision, to be sure, has value if you observe the law; but if you break the law, your circumcision has become uncircumcision. [26]Again, if an uncircumcised man keeps the precepts of the law, will he not be considered circumcised? [27]Indeed, those who are physically uncircumcised but carry out the law will pass judgment on you, with your written law and circumcision, who break the law. [28]One is not a Jew outwardly. True circumcision is not outward, in the flesh. [29]Rather, one is a Jew inwardly, and circumcision is of the heart, in the spirit, not the letter; his praise is not from human beings but from God.

3 Answers to Objections. [1]What advantage is there then in being a Jew? Or what is the value of circumcision? [2]Much, in every respect. [For] in the first place, they were entrusted with

arms, for they mistakenly thought that Powers was attacking them, whereas he was pointing his literary finger at people, lay or clergy, who were greedy, self-centered, and lazy.

A compelling parallel to what Paul is doing in this passage occurs in what Epictetus writes in his discourse: "To those who take up the teachings of the philosophers only to talk about them." Epictetus addresses the would-be teacher, whose deeds are evil: "For your own evils are enough for you: your baseness, your cowardice, the bragging that you indulged in when you were sitting in the lecture room. Why did you pride yourself on things that were not your own?" (*Discourses* 2.19.19, in Loeb translation). Instead of teaching Gentiles the true way to God, this vain teacher leads them away from God. Indeed, Isaiah 52:5 is verified here, for the Gentiles revile God's name because of what the Jewish teacher has done or failed to do.

3:1-9 God's chosen people, although sinners, are still advantaged

Paul continues his scholastic diatribe with a series of five objections or questions. Each objection is twofold. See 3:1, 3, 5, 7-8a, 9a for these questions and 3:2, 4, 6, 8b, and 9b for Paul's responses. Although this series of

the utterances of God. ³What if some were unfaithful? Will their infidelity nullify the fidelity of God? ⁴Of course not! God must be true, though every human being is a liar, as it is written:

"That you may be justified in your words,
and conquer when you are judged."

⁵But if our wickedness provides proof of God's righteousness, what can we say? Is God unjust, humanly speaking, to inflict his wrath? ⁶Of course not! For how else is God to judge the world? ⁷But if God's truth redounds to his glory through my falsehood, why am I still being condemned as a sinner? ⁸And why not say—as we are accused and as some claim we say—that we should do evil that good may come of it? Their penalty is what they deserve.

Universal Bondage to Sin. ⁹Well, then, are we better off? Not entirely, for we have already brought the charge against Jews and Greeks alike that they are all under the domination of sin, ¹⁰as it is written:

---

questions and answers functions very well here, it is a foretaste of Paul's extensive discussion in Romans 9–11 about God's fidelity in the face of the nonbelief in Jesus the Christ on the part of most of the chosen people.

I focus on Paul's responses in 3:4 and 3:6 and then on both question and answer in 3:9. Romans 3:4 reads: "God must be true." God's truthfulness refers to God's covenant fidelity to the chosen people. See Psalm 89:2: "The promises of the LORD I will sing forever, / proclaim your loyalty [truthfulness] through all ages." Romans 3:6 proclaims that God is judge of the world. Psalm 94:2 pleads with God: "Rise up, judge of the earth; / give the proud what they deserve." Romans 3:9a is surely a difficult sentence, especially since the antecedent "we" of 3:8 is ambiguous. If the "we" includes both Paul and his imaginary Jewish interlocutor, then the translation is: "What then? Are we [Jews] disadvantaged? Not at all." If the "we" refers solely to Paul, then F. W. Danker's translation makes sense: "What then? Am I protecting myself? Am I making excuses? Not at all."

Readers should not miss the occurrence of the noun "sin" for the first time in Romans 3:9b. Through the use of personification, Paul paints sin as a master who dominates Jew and Gentile. What irony for those who believed they had achieved self-mastery.

3:10-20 Observance of the law does not lead to justification

If my readers have an image of Paul rapidly dictating this letter to his scribe Tertius (see 16:22), this passage should cause a drastic revision of that image. For nowhere in Scripture are these ten quotations found together

"There is no one just, not one,
 ¹¹there is no one who understands,
  there is no one who seeks
    God.
¹²All have gone astray; all alike are
   worthless;
  there is not one who does good,
   [there is not] even one.
¹³Their throats are open graves;
  they deceive with their tongues;
the venom of asps is on their lips;
 ¹⁴their mouths are full of bitter
   cursing.
¹⁵Their feet are quick to shed blood;
 ¹⁶ruin and misery are in their
   ways,
¹⁷and the way of peace they know
   not.
 ¹⁸There is no fear of God before
   their eyes."

¹⁹Now we know that what the law says is addressed to those under the law, so that every mouth may be silenced and the whole world stand accountable to God, ²⁰since no human being will be justified in his sight by observing the law; for through the law comes consciousness of sin.

III. Justification through
Faith in Christ

Justification apart from the Law.
²¹But now the righteousness of God has been manifested apart from the law, though testified to by the law and the prophets, ²²the righteousness of God through faith in Jesus Christ for all who believe. For there is no distinction; ²³all have sinned and are deprived of the

---

in the same book. They seem to have been composed beforehand. Take 3:13, for example. "Their throats are open graves; / they deceive with their tongues" (author's translation) is found in the Septuagint of Psalm 5:10. The next line of 3:13, however, comes from the Septuagint of Psalm 139:4: "The venom of asps is on their lips." The motif of "no one, not one" surges through 3:10-12, and the full involvement of the human person (from head to toe) seems to be the ordering principle for 3:13-18.

Paul's long chain of Scripture quotations should not distract us from the conclusion he draws in 3:20: "No human being will be justified in his [God's] sight by observing the law." That is, neither the chosen people nor the Gentiles find justification in the law. Romans 3:21-26 will state where justification may now be found.

JUSTIFICATION THROUGH FAITH IN CHRIST

Romans 3:21–5:21

3:21-26 The soteriological heart of Romans

Having argued his thesis by means of its antithesis in 1:18–3:20, Paul now formulates it positively in a section that is soteriologically and christologically significant but dense. I highlight five key points and leave to

glory of God. [24]They are justified freely by his grace through the redemption in Christ Jesus, [25]whom God set forth as an expiation, through faith, by his blood, to prove his righteousness because of the forgiveness of sins previously committed, [26]through the forbearance of God—to prove his righteousness in the present time, that he might be righteous and justify the one who has faith in Jesus.

[27]What occasion is there then for boasting? It is ruled out. On what principle, that of works? No, rather on the

---

advanced students an investigation of the likelihood that Paul adapted earlier tradition in 3:24-26. First, the law does not bring about justification, although it testifies to it (3:21). Paul will address the role of the law in Romans 4 and 7–11, for "the law is holy, and the commandment is holy and righteous and good" (7:12).

Second, "[all sinners] are justified freely" (3:24), that is, God has declared them to be acquitted of their sin.

Third, Christ's death on the cross is front and center stage in the words "by his blood" (3:25). Christ's shedding of his blood has brought about redemption, an image that denotes being ransomed from the slavery and domination of sin (see 3:9).

Fourth, 3:25 employs another image—that of expiation. God has set forth Jesus Christ on the cross as the new expiatory sacrifice that takes away sin through the shedding of his blood. The Old Testament background seems to be Exodus 25:17 ("You shall then make an expiating cover") and Leviticus 16:15-16: "Then he (Aaron) shall slaughter the people's sin-offering goat, and bringing its blood inside the veil, he shall do with it as he did with the bullock's blood, sprinkling it on the expiatory and before it. Thus he shall make atonement for the sanctuary because of all the sinful defilements and faults of the Israelites" (author's translations).

Fifth, four times in this passage "faith" or "to believe" occurs (3:22). Justification, redemption, expiation are not forced upon men and women. They have to respond in faith to God who has done these things for them through Jesus Christ.

3:27–4:2a A person is justified by faith

This section is yet another dialogue in diatribe modality. In it Paul leads his readers to appreciate the centrality of faith for both Jew and Gentile. God who is one does not require two ways but only one—that of faith. The section begins with "boasting," ends with "boasting," and leads to the example of Abraham (4:2b-25), whose faith was credited to him as righteousness (4:9).

principle of faith. [28]For we consider that a person is justified by faith apart from works of the law. [29]Does God belong to Jews alone? Does he not belong to Gentiles, too? Yes, also to Gentiles, [30]for God is one and will justify the circumcised on the basis of faith and the uncircumcised through faith. [31]Are we then annulling the law by this faith? Of course not! On the contrary, we are supporting the law.

Abraham Justified by Faith. [1]What then can we say that Abraham found, our ancestor according to the flesh? [2]Indeed, if Abraham was justified on the basis of his works, he has reason to boast; but this was not so in the sight of God. [3]For what does the scripture say? "Abraham believed God, and it was credited to him as righteousness." [4]A worker's wage is credited not as a gift, but as something due. [5]But

I lay out this dialogue, modifying the NAB translation above and indicating the interlocutor by "I" and Paul by "P." Paul formulates the interlocutor's questions in such a way as to lead to his key theological teachings.

I: Is there reason to boast?

P: It is ruled out.

I: By what principle? That of the law?

P: No, rather by the principle of faith. For we consider that a person is justified by faith apart from works of the law. Does God belong only to Jews? Does he not belong also to Gentiles?

I: Yes, also to Gentiles.

P: For God is one and will justify the circumcised on the basis of faith and the uncircumcised through faith.

I: Are we then annulling the law by faith?

P: Of course not. On the contrary, we are supporting the law.

I: What then are we to say? Have we found Abraham, to be our forebear by his own efforts? For if Abraham was justified on the basis of his works, he has reason to boast.

All of Romans 4:2b-25 will give Paul's response: Faithful Abraham has no reason to boast.

4:2b-25 Abraham's faith and the God who justifies the ungodly

Romans 4:2b-25 provides Paul's reasons why Abraham has no reason to boast: he did nothing to earn justification. Put positively and compactly, Abraham, a Gentile, believed God despite all evidence to the contrary. In

when one does not work, yet believes in the one who justifies the ungodly, his faith is credited as righteousness. ⁶So also David declares the blessedness of the person to whom God credits righteousness apart from works:

> ⁷"Blessed are they whose iniquities
>   are forgiven
>   and whose sins are covered.
> ⁸Blessed is the man whose sin the
>   Lord does not record."

⁹Does this blessedness apply only to the circumcised, or to the uncircumcised as well? Now we assert that "faith was credited to Abraham as righteousness." ¹⁰Under what circumstances was it credited? Was he circumcised or not? He was not circumcised, but uncircumcised. ¹¹And he received the sign of circumcision as a seal on the righteousness received through faith while he was uncircumcised. Thus he was to be

---

fashioning his final answer to the diatribal dialogue that commenced in 3:27, Paul utilizes another feature of the scholastic diatribe: teaching by means of examples. For instance, Epictetus draws upon luminaries of the philosophical tradition such as Plato, Diogenes, and Epicurus to paint positive and negative examples. Paul reaches back into the Jewish tradition to forebear Abraham. It is very important to note what characteristics of Abraham are of theological interest to Paul and what Abraham's example says about God.

Recall what Paul says about the sins of the Gentiles in 1:18-32. Abraham was a Gentile, an idolater, an ungodly person when God called him out of Ur of Chaldea. Drawing upon Genesis 15:16, Paul notes: "Abraham believed God, and it was credited to him as righteousness" (Rom 4:3). Abraham hadn't undergone the rite of circumcision when he believed (Gen 17). Nor was he being rewarded for having offered gracious and generous hospitality to strangers (Gen 18). He had not yet been obedient to God in his willingness to sacrifice his only son, Isaac, the carrier of God's praises (Gen 22). Abraham was the recipient of a gift (Rom 4:4). Why did God do this? The reason is found in God's nature: God justifies the ungodly (4:5). Earlier, in 3:10-18, Paul displayed one of his ways of interpreting Scripture as he strung together quotations from various parts of Scripture in a chain. In 4:7-8 Paul follows another method, namely, citing a Scripture passage that contains the same key word. Both of these passages, then, interpret each other. In this instance Paul quotes Psalm 31:1-2 in the Septuagint because it contains the same key verb "to credit." The NAB's "does not record" (4:8) masks this point. Through God's act of justification, God forgives iniquities. In 4:9-12 Paul draws yet another point from Abraham's faith: Through his faith Abraham is the father of both the uncircumcised and the circumcised.

the father of all the uncircumcised who believe, so that to them [also] righteousness might be credited, [12]as well as the father of the circumcised who not only are circumcised, but also follow the path of faith that our father Abraham walked while still uncircumcised.

Inheritance through Faith. [13]It was not through the law that the promise was made to Abraham and his descendants that he would inherit the world, but through the righteousness that comes from faith. [14]For if those who adhere to the law are the heirs, faith is null and the promise is void. [15]For the law produces wrath; but where there is no law, neither is there violation. [16]For this reason, it depends on faith, so that it may be a gift, and the promise may be guaranteed to all his descendants, not to those who only adhere to the law but to those who follow the faith of Abraham, who is the father of all of us, [17]as it is written, "I have made you father of many nations." He is our father in the sight of God, in whom he believed, who gives life to the dead and calls into being what does not exist. [18]He believed, hoping against hope, that he would become "the father of many nations," according to what was said, "Thus shall your descendants be." [19]He did not weaken in faith when he considered his own body as [already] dead (for he was almost a hundred years old) and the dead womb of Sarah. [20]He did not doubt God's promise in unbelief; rather, he was empowered by faith and gave glory to God [21]and was fully convinced that what he had promised he was also able to do. [22]That is why "it was credited to him as righteousness." [23]But it was not for him alone that it was written that "it was credited to him"; [24]it was also for us, to whom it will be credited, who believe in the one who

---

In Romans 7–8 Paul will pay close attention to, and argue extensively about, the role of the law. In 4:13-16 Paul whets his hearers' appetites with apodictic statements, the key of which is: "If those who adhere to the law are the heirs, faith is null and the promise is void" (4:14).

In 4:17-22 Paul moves away from his earlier, more abstract consideration of Abraham as a model of faith and gets specific. Again Paul confesses a cardinal point of his and our faith: God "who gives life to the dead and calls into being what does not exist" (4:17). Through this faith Abraham was empowered to trust God's word and promise. Abraham's God has given life to his almost dead body and to the dead womb of his wife, Sarah. In 4:23-25 Paul moves from Abraham's faith in the God who justifies the ungodly and gives life to the dead and draws himself and his hearers into the story. Notice the change of personal pronouns in 4:24-25: "It was also for *us . . . our* Lord . . . for *our* transgressions . . . for *our* justification" (emphasis added).

Scholars who interpret Romans from a story perspective have hit pay dirt in Romans 4. The story of Abraham and Sarah captivates believers,

raised Jesus our Lord from the dead, [25]who was handed over for our transgressions and was raised for our justification.

5 **Faith, Hope, and Love.** [1]Therefore, since we have been justified by faith, we have peace with God through our Lord Jesus Christ, [2]through whom we have gained access [by faith] to this grace in which we stand, and we boast in hope of the glory of God. [3]Not only that, but we even boast of our afflictions, knowing that affliction produces endurance, [4]and endurance, proven character, and proven character, hope, [5]and hope does not disappoint, because the love of God has been poured out into our hearts through the holy Spirit that has been given to us. [6]For Christ, while we were still helpless, yet died at the appointed time for the ungodly. [7]Indeed, only with difficulty does one die for a just person, though perhaps for a good person one might even find courage to die. [8]But God proves his love for us in that while we were still sinners Christ died for us. [9]How much more then, since we are now justified by his blood, will we be saved through him from the wrath. [10]Indeed, if, while we were enemies, we were reconciled to God through the death of his Son,

who are led to see in these forebears their stories of hoping against hope (4:18), believing that God draws life out of death and trusting that God justifies ungodly people such as us who may have been overcome by sin.

5:1-11 God's many gifts through Jesus Christ our Lord

This is an exceedingly rich passage. I offer six considerations. First, I urge my readers to note Paul's use of "we." I count seventeen uses of "we/our." I would venture to say that Paul is including himself with his Gentile hearers, and his main purpose is *pathos*. In my Introduction (p. 40) I stated that the author experiences the emotion that he wants his listeners to experience. In this passage the "emotions" are the entire gambit of God's gifts: peace, love, boasting, hope, reconciliation, the Holy Spirit.

Second, in this passage Paul often makes reference to teachings he presented earlier. Boasting (5:2, 3, 11), which Paul and his society considered good as long as it was done decently, stands in stark contrast with the illegitimate boasting of 3:17 and 4:2 and ties this passage to what preceded it. Because of God's many gifts, the Gentiles can toot their own horn, and do so to God's honor. The peace (5:1) that the Gentiles are experiencing is not that created by Caesar Augustus but by Jesus Christ our Lord (see 1:7). In 1:16 Paul proudly proclaimed that he was not ashamed of the gospel of Jesus Christ, crucified as a criminal but raised by God from the dead. Romans 5:5 contains the same verb "to shame": Hope does not shame because of the reality of God's gift of absolutely gratuitous love (see 5:5).

how much more, once reconciled, will we be saved by his life. [11]Not only that, but we also boast of God through our Lord Jesus Christ, through whom we have now received reconciliation.

Humanity's Sin through Adam. [12]Therefore, just as through one person sin entered the world, and through sin, death, and thus death came to all, inasmuch as all sinned—[13]for up to the time of the law, sin was in the world, though sin is not accounted when there is no law. [14]But death reigned from Adam to Moses, even over those who did not sin after the pattern of the trespass of Adam, who is the type of the one who was to come.

Grace and Life through Christ. [15]But the gift is not like the transgression. For if by that one person's transgression the many died, how much more did the grace of God and the gracious gift of the one person Jesus Christ overflow for the many. [16]And the gift is not like the result of the one person's sinning. For after one sin there was the judgment that brought condemnation; but the gift, after many transgressions, brought ac-

---

Third, in 5:3-5, Paul displays his literary prowess as he fashions a *sorites* (literally: "a heap"), as he moves from affliction to endurance to proven character to hope.

Four, notice how many times Paul refers to Jesus Christ (5:1, 2, 6, 8, 9, 10, 11). Jesus Christ is God's Son (5:10). Through the shedding of his blood we have reconciliation with God, that is, enemies have turned their tanks into plows. In Jewish tradition there is the story of a mother and seven sons who resisted the tyrant Antiochus and preserved their faith and ancestral customs, even though they were mercilessly tortured and killed for their fidelity. Their deaths were of great benefit to the entire nation. 4 Maccabees 17:22 reads: "Through the blood of these devout ones and their death as an atoning sacrifice, divine Providence preserved Israel which had previously been mistreated" (NRSV modified). Jesus' death is of even greater benefit to humanity.

Fifth, the multiple gifts that Gentile believers experience do not come from their own inner strength but through God's Spirit, who is other and holy (5:5).

Finally, Paul's "how much more" argument in 5:10 prepares his hearers for his argument in 5:12-21. See, for example, 5:15. God's gifts through Jesus Christ enable people to attain the self-mastery that they and their culture have been longing for.

5:12-21 The wondrous consequences of the obedience of Jesus Christ

In Romans 5:12 the "we" style vanishes (except for the use of "our" in the formulaic ending of 5:21: "through Jesus Christ *our* Lord"; emphasis

quittal. ¹⁷For if, by the transgression of one person, death came to reign through that one, how much more will those who receive the abundance of grace and of the gift of justification come to reign in life through the one person Jesus Christ. ¹⁸In conclusion, just as through one transgression condemnation came upon all, so through one righteous act acquittal and life came to all. ¹⁹For just as through the disobedience of one person the many were made sinners, so through the obedience of one the many will be made righteous. ²⁰The law entered in so that transgression might increase but, where sin increased, grace overflowed all the more, ²¹so that, as sin reigned in death, grace also might reign through

added), and Paul adopts the discursive third person style. If you ask how 5:12-21 connects with what has preceded, I give two answers. It gives an analysis of sin that is more profound than that given in 1:18–3:20. Further, it praises the wondrous gifts that have come about through the faithful obedience of Jesus Christ and thus continues the general thematic of 5:1-11. Paul may have composed this passage on another occasion and saw how fitting it was for this letter.

It is important to quote two Scripture passages as background to Romans 5:12-14. Genesis 2:16-17 states: "The LORD God gave man this order: 'You are free to eat from any of the trees of the garden except the tree of knowledge of good and bad. From that tree you shall not eat; the moment you eat from it you are surely doomed to die'" (NAB). Adam's sin of disobedience brings about death. Wisdom 2:23-24 speaks of the reign of death: "For God formed man to be imperishable; / the image of his own nature he made him. / But by the envy of the devil, death entered the world, / and they who are in his possession experience it" (NAB). As Luke Timothy Johnson writes: "Everyone has sinned the way Adam did, so that the effect of Adam's sin continues, and continues to be symbolized by the death experienced by all humans."

But as Paul teaches through the extensive comparisons of 5:15-21, Adam's disobedience is not the end of the story. Paul makes his point much more succinctly in 1 Corinthians 15:45: "So, too, it is written, 'The first man, Adam, became a living being,' the last Adam a life-giving spirit." The risen Lord Jesus stands at the beginning of the new creation. While on the side of Adam are disobedience, transgression, and death, on the side of the New Adam there are obedience, acquittal, life, and grace. "In conclusion, just as through one transgression condemnation came upon all, so through one righteous act acquittal and life came to all" (5:18). In Romans 6–8 Paul will spell out the meaning of incorporation into the

justification for eternal life through Jesus Christ our Lord.

IV. Justification and the Christian Life

6 **Freedom from Sin; Life in God.** [1]What then shall we say? Shall we persist in sin that grace may abound? Of course not! [2]How can we who died to sin yet live in it? [3]Or are you un-aware that we who were baptized into Christ Jesus were baptized into his death? [4]We were indeed buried with him through baptism into death, so that, just as Christ was raised from the dead by the glory of the Father, we too might live in newness of life.

[5]For if we have grown into union with him through a death like his, we shall also be united with him in the

life of the New Adam through baptism (Rom 6), the role of the law (Rom 7), and the driving force of God's Spirit (Rom 8).

Advocates of the story approach to Romans are happy that Paul has finally shown the narrative that lies below the surface of his discursive soteriology and christology. Jesus, God's Son, has redeemed believers not from one single sin but from the power of sin and death. Those who experienced the power of Osama bin Ladin on 9/11/01 have no doubt that the transgression of one single individual has a negative effect on millions. Even the musical *Beauty and the Beast* teaches us that the selfish, heartless action of one individual has consequences for an entire household. On the positive side, the narrative of the life of Francis of Assisi (d. 1226) continues to breathe fresh life into countless people of all faiths.

JUSTIFICATION AND THE CHRISTIAN LIFE

Romans 6:1–8:39

6:1-14 Baptism and the newness of life

Paul develops the points he has been making in Romans 5:12-21 by means of an objection by an imaginary interlocutor in 6:1-2. Throughout 6:2-14, Paul will be answering the absurd question of 6:1: "Shall we persist in sin that grace may abound?" The attentive reader will note Paul's use of "we" in 6:1-9 and his use of "you" plural in 6:11-14. What the Gentile believers in Romans experienced in baptism Paul also experienced. Thus Paul engages in *pathos* or exhorting his hearers on the basis of common experience. Finally, from his description of baptism (6:2-5), Paul will draw upon some common principles (6:6-10) and then apply them (6:11-14).

The ritual of infant baptism and especially the baptism of adults at the Easter Vigil give us some inkling of Paul's view of baptism. The immersion

61

Part of the Roman Forum, the center of trade, religion, and politics in ancient Rome. To the right is the Temple of Antoninus and Faustina, converted into a church in the Middle Ages.

resurrection. [6]We know that our old self was crucified with him, so that our sinful body might be done away with, that we might no longer be in slavery to sin. [7]For a dead person has been absolved from sin. [8]If, then, we have died with Christ, we believe that we shall also live with him. [9]We know that Christ, raised from the dead, dies no more; death no longer has power over him. [10]As to his death, he died to sin once and for all; as to his life, he lives for God. [11]Consequently, you too must think of yourselves as [being] dead to sin and living for God in Christ Jesus.

[12]Therefore, sin must not reign over your mortal bodies so that you obey their desires. [13]And do not present the parts of your bodies to sin as weapons for wickedness, but present yourselves to God as raised from the dead to life and the parts of your bodies to God as weapons for righteousness. [14]For sin is not to have any power over you, since you are not under the law but under grace.

---

of the baptizand is likened to Christ's death and burial; the lifting up out of the water is likened to Christ's resurrection. The change of clothing points to the newly baptized's change of status.

Although I have been trying to interpret Romans without explicit reference to Galatians, I believe that some verses from this earlier letter help us to appreciate what Paul means here by baptism. Galatians 3:1-5 very clearly points to the explosive nature of the Christian experience of baptism. See especially Galatians 3:5: "Does, then, the one who supplies the Spirit to you and works mighty deeds among you do so from works of the law or from faith in what you heard?" Baptism may very well have been the occasion for the display of the multiple gifts of the Spirit (see 1 Cor 12–14), the time when the love of God was manifestly "poured out into our hearts through the holy Spirit" (Rom 5:5) and the time when the newly baptized cried out "Abba, Father!" (Gal 4:6; Rom 8:15) as a profession of their new status as children of God.

Romans 6:6-10 largely consists of "principles." Paul's use of "for" in 6:5, 7 announces principles. For example, 6:7 states that the person who has died has lost the very means of sinning, namely, "our sinful body" (6:6). The "if" sentences of 6:5, 8 formulate principles. The "we know" sentences of 6:6, 9 remind listeners of principles.

Romans 6:11-14 applies these principles to Paul's Gentile listeners, who were quite aware of the vices that dominated their society (see Rom 1:18-32). "Therefore, sin must not reign over your mortal bodies so that you obey their desires" (6:12). In Romans 8 Paul will spend considerable time on the role of the Holy Spirit in believers' everyday lives of living out the newness of baptismal life.

¹⁵What then? Shall we sin because we are not under the law but under grace? Of course not! ¹⁶Do you not know that if you present yourselves to someone as obedient slaves, you are slaves of the one you obey, either of sin, which leads to death, or of obedience, which leads to righteousness? ¹⁷But thanks be to God that, although you were once slaves of sin, you have become obedient from the heart to the pattern of teaching to which you were entrusted. ¹⁸Freed from sin, you have become slaves of righteousness. ¹⁹I am speaking in human terms because of the weakness of your nature. For just as you presented the parts of your bodies as slaves to impurity and to lawlessness for lawlessness, so now present them as slaves to righteousness for sanctification. ²⁰For when you were slaves of sin, you were free from righteousness.

6:15-23 Be addicted to the Lord Jesus Christ

Paul develops his teaching some more by means of another rhetorical question in the first person: "What then? Shall we sin because we are not under the law but under grace? Of course not!" (6:15). With the exception of 6:19, where Paul uses "I," this entire section is in the second person and is addressed to Gentile believers who once engaged in sins of which they are now ashamed (6:21; see 1:24-28).

To me, the best contemporary analogy to the master-slave relationship that Paul utilizes in this section is addiction. We all know of individuals who are addicted to gambling or alcohol or drugs and will do just about anything to get their daily "fix." These individuals are in thralldom, in slavery to their addiction. Even though they realize in their sober moments that they are destroying their lives and those of the people they love, they cannot help themselves. They are very clever at hiding their addiction and at making excuses for their conduct.

If we apply this analogy to 6:16-23, we realize that because of all that God has done for us in Jesus Christ—justification, redemption, gift of the Holy Spirit, baptism—we are now to be addicted to righteousness, sanctification, and life. We are to be "obedient from the heart to the pattern of teaching to which [we] were entrusted" (6:17). The reference here is most likely to the core of teaching given at the time of baptism in the midst of one's brothers and sisters. In 6:19, 22 Paul introduces a new term, "sanctification." Just as their God is holy or "other," the lives of believers are to be "other." How "other"? Paul's reference back to the sins of Romans 1:18-32 gives a glimpse of what has to be left behind in believers' new addiction to Jesus Christ.

This section ends with a rousing summary: "The wages of sin is death, but the gift of God is eternal life in Christ Jesus our Lord"(6:23). I conclude

²¹But what profit did you get then from the things of which you are now ashamed? For the end of those things is death. ²²But now that you have been freed from sin and have become slaves of God, the benefit that you have leads to sanctification, and its end is eternal life. ²³For the wages of sin is death, but the gift of God is eternal life in Christ Jesus our Lord.

7 Freedom from the Law. ¹Are you unaware, brothers (for I am speaking to people who know the law), that the law has jurisdiction over one as long as one lives? ²Thus a married woman is bound by law to her living husband; but if her husband dies, she is released from the law in respect to her husband. ³Consequently, while her husband is alive she will be called an adulteress if

by accentuating the plural number of the "you" that Paul employs in this section. Individuals do not come out of addiction by themselves. They need outside help, community, loved ones. In this instance, they need the Christian community or local house church.

7:1-6 The role of the law: Part I

As Paul has been making his case that new life in Christ has freed believers from the power of sin and death, he has often dropped hints about the role of the Mosaic law. I mention some of Paul's earlier pronouncements about the law. See 3:20: "no human being will be justified in his sight by observing the law; for through the law comes consciousness of sin." In Romans 4:14-15 Paul states: "For if those who adhere to the law are the heirs, faith is null and the promise is void. For the law produces wrath; but where there is no law, neither is there violation." After mentioning the law in 5:13, Paul says in 5:20: "The law entered in so that transgression might increase but, where sin increased, grace overflowed all the more." Finally, Romans 6:14-15 reads: "For sin is not to have any power over you, since you are not under the law but under grace. What then? Shall we sin because we are not under the law but under grace?" These hints have whetted our appetites. Now Paul sets the table for a full course on the law.

Again, I invite my readers to check Paul's personal pronouns. Romans 7:2-3 is an illustration in the third person. Romans 7:1 and 4 have "you" plural and the fictive kinship term "brothers [and sisters]." Romans 7:4c-6 employs "we" pronouns as Paul identifies himself with his Gentile hearers.

The illustration is pretty straightforward, as it talks about the binding force of law for a married couple while both partners are alive. It presupposes that this married union will result in the bearing of fruit (children; see 7:4-5). Once the husband has died, the law of marriage for the wife ceases. She is free to marry another.

she consorts with another man. But if her husband dies she is free from that law, and she is not an adulteress if she consorts with another man.

⁴In the same way, my brothers, you also were put to death to the law through the body of Christ, so that you might belong to another, to the one who was raised from the dead in order that we might bear fruit for God. ⁵For when we were in the flesh, our sinful passions, awakened by the law, worked in our members to bear fruit for death. ⁶But now we are released from the law, dead to what held us captive, so that we may serve in the newness of the spirit and not under the obsolete letter.

Acquaintance with Sin through the Law. ⁷What then can we say? That the law is sin? Of course not! Yet I did not

Paul introduces the application of this illustration by the words "in the same way" in 7:4, but note the ways in which he transfers the terms of the illustration. See, for example, 7:4: "You also were put to death to the law through the [crucified] body of Christ, so that you might belong to another, to the one who was raised from the dead in order that we might bear fruit for God." It is clear that believers now belong to another, namely, Jesus Christ. It is also clear that the death of Jesus Christ has destroyed the power of law over believers. When we were without the Spirit, that is, in the flesh (see Romans 8 for more detail), the law awakened sinful passions by forbidding certain actions. Like people caught in a bad marriage, we were held captive to destructive forces. But now that the law is dead, we may serve "in the newness of the spirit" (7:6).

7:7–8:2 The role of the law: Part II

Paul develops his thought here about the relationship between law and sin by means of two diatribal objections and answers in 7:7a and 7:13a. Each answer is developed further in what follows. I am indebted to Stanley Stowers for the interpretation that the "I" that occurs in virtually every verse of 7:7-25 is an instance of what the Greeks called *prosopopoiia*, or "speech in character." Finally, 7:25a and 8:1-2 are Paul's remarks to the "I."

Speech in character "is a rhetorical and literary technique in which the speaker or writer produces speech that represents not himself or herself but another person or type of character." Thus the "I" is not Paul nor a Jew nor a Christian; rather the "I" is the Gentile striving to attain self-mastery by means of observance of the Mosaic law. In his own way, Joseph A. Fitzmyer is on the same wavelength as Stowers when he comments that the "I" is: "unregenerate humanity faced with the Mosaic law—but as seen by a Christian."

65

know sin except through the law, and I did not know what it is to covet except that the law said, "You shall not covet." ⁸But sin, finding an opportunity in the commandment, produced in me every kind of covetousness. Apart from the law sin is dead. ⁹I once lived outside the law, but when the commandment came, sin became alive; ¹⁰then I died, and the commandment that was for life turned out to be death for me. ¹¹For sin, seizing an opportunity in the commandment, deceived me and through it put me to death. ¹²So then the law is holy, and the commandment is holy and righteous and good.

Sin and Death. ¹³Did the good, then, become death for me? Of course not! Sin, in order that it might be shown to be sin, worked death in me through the

---

Key verses in this interpretation are 7:15 and 7:19, which are paralleled in Greek literature and philosophy. Romans 7:15 reads: "What I do, I do not understand. For I do not do what I want, but I do what I hate." Romans 7:19 states: "For I do not do the good I want, but I do the evil I do not want." Such was the situation of Medea in Greek tragedy, who, overcome by anger and the desire for revenge, killed her own children. In Euripides' *Medea* the main character wails: "I am overcome by evil. Now, now, I learn what horrors I intend, but passion overpowers sober thought, and this is the cause of the direst evils for men and women" (1077–1080; Loeb modified). Medea, a pagan, is the model for lack of self-mastery.

There is a heart-rending version of Medea in Samuel Barber's "Medea's Dance of Vengeance." See also the Roman poet Ovid, who in his *Metamorphoses* comments: "I see the better and approve it, but I follow the worse" (7.20-21; Loeb). In his *Discourses* the Stoic philosopher Epictetus writes: "What he wants to do he doesn't do, and what he doesn't want he does" (2, 26.4; Loeb modified).

Into this pagan situation of being mastered by the passions, Jewish apologists such as Philo of Alexandria proclaimed that the Jewish Mosaic law made Jews more self-controlled, better able to control their passions. In Book IV.55 of his *Special Laws*, Philo praises the Mosaic law: "The law thinks that all those who adhere to the sacred constitution, established by Moses, ought to be free from all unreasonable passions, and from all wickedness" (C. D. Yonge translation).

Paul agrees that "the law is holy, and the commandment is holy and righteous and good" (7:12). But he also realizes that sin has overwhelmed the law: "For sin, seizing an opportunity in the commandment, deceived me and through it put me to death" (7:11). If Gentiles cannot turn to the Mosaic law for liberation from the powers of sin, death, and flesh, they must turn and have turned to Jesus Christ. Before the "I" of the "speech in

good, so that sin might become sinful beyond measure through the commandment. [14]We know that the law is spiritual; but I am carnal, sold into slavery to sin. [15]What I do, I do not understand. For I do not do what I want, but I do what I hate. [16]Now if I do what I do not want, I concur that the law is good. [17]So now it is no longer I who do it, but sin that dwells in me. [18]For I know that good does not dwell in me, that is, in my flesh. The willing is ready at hand, but doing the good is not. [19]For I do not do the good I want, but I do the evil I do not want. [20]Now if [I] do what I do not want, it is no longer I who do it, but sin that dwells in me. [21]So, then, I discover the principle that when I want to do right, evil is at hand. [22]For I take delight in the law of God, in my inner self, [23]but I see in my members another principle at war with the law of my mind, taking me captive to the law of sin that dwells in my members. [24]Miserable one that I am! Who will deliver me from this mortal body? [25]Thanks be to God through Jesus Christ our Lord. Therefore, I myself, with my mind, serve the law of God but, with my flesh, the law of sin.

The Flesh and the Spirit. [1]Hence, now there is no condemnation for those who are in Christ Jesus. [2]For the law of the spirit of life in Christ Jesus has freed you from the law of sin and death. [3]For what the law, weakened by the flesh, was powerless to do, this God has done: by sending his own Son in

character" has a chance to complete its tale of woe and misery, Paul, the author of this letter, interrupts and exclaims: "Thanks be to God through Jesus Christ our Lord" (7:25a).

In Romans 8:1-2 the author Paul again returns from using "speech in character" and in 8:2 addresses the "I," now turned to "you" singular: "For the law of the spirit of life in Christ Jesus has freed *you* from the law of sin and death" (emphasis added). That is, Paul does not immediately turn to the hearers of his letter by using "you" plural. He is completing his theological thought and captivating his hearers by using the artistry of "speech in character."

8:3-13 The life of God's Spirit in the believer

All of Romans 8 addresses the question: If the law is unable to give life, then whence comes life? In this section Paul answers this question by pointing to the Gentile believers' experience of the Spirit. I invite my readers to once again look carefully at the pronouns in this section. Although "us" occurs in 8:4, I would suggest that 8:12 contains the key "we" statement: "Consequently, brothers [and sisters], we are not debtors to the flesh, to live according to the flesh." Paul expresses his teaching about the flesh and the Spirit in the third person in 8:5-8. Romans 8:9-11, 13 captures the attention of Paul's Gentile listeners at Rome, as Paul uses "you" plural. Self-mastery

the likeness of sinful flesh and for the sake of sin, he condemned sin in the flesh, [4]so that the righteous decree of the law might be fulfilled in us, who live not according to the flesh but according to the spirit. [5]For those who live according to the flesh are concerned with the things of the flesh, but those who live according to the spirit with the things of the spirit. [6]The concern of the flesh is death, but the concern of the spirit is life and peace. [7]For the concern of the flesh is hostility toward God; it does not submit to the law of God, nor can it; [8]and those who are in the flesh cannot please God. [9]But you are not in the flesh; on the contrary, you are in the spirit, if only the Spirit of God dwells in you. Whoever does not have the Spirit of Christ does not belong to him. [10]But if Christ is in you, although the body is dead because of sin, the spirit is alive because of righteousness. [11]If the Spirit of the one who raised Jesus from the dead dwells in you, the one who raised Christ from the dead will give life to your mortal bodies also, through his Spirit that dwells in you. [12]Consequently, brothers, we are not debtors to the flesh, to live according to the flesh. [13]For if you live according to the flesh, you will die, but if by the spirit you put to death the deeds of the body, you will live.

Children of God through Adoption. [14]For those who are led by the Spirit of God are children of God. [15]For you did

---

does not come from the law but from the Spirit. Romans 8:13b reads: "If by the spirit you put to death the deeds of the body, you will live."

For the rest I focus on two points. Romans 8:3 contains a lapidary statement about Paul's view of God, who has given life to believers by "sending his own Son in the likeness of sinful flesh and for the sake of sin." God's own Son has become human and through his death has taken away humanity's sin. My second point deals with Paul's contrast between flesh and Spirit. For Paul "the flesh" is not to be confused or equated with sexual sins. "The flesh" is the entire human person, turned away from God and turned toward self. Paul's discussion of the flesh and the Spirit in Galatians 5:19-23 is very illuminating. In Galatians 5:19-21 Paul lists among "the works of the flesh" such human intellectual and willful actions as "idolatry, sorcery, . . . envy, . . . acts of selfishness." For Paul, "the Spirit" comprises God's actions toward the world, God's presence in the world, for God's people, in a creative way. Galatians 5:22-23 is very enlightening, for Paul lists among "the fruit of the Spirit" such creative actions as "love, . . . generosity, . . . self-control."

8:14-30 The future of believers is now

I formulate the theme that courses through this long section in this way: What believers experience now is the foretaste, the firstfruits, the down payment of what is to come. In more technical terminology, Paul

not receive a spirit of slavery to fall back into fear, but you received a spirit of adoption, through which we cry, "*Abba*, Father!" ¹⁶The Spirit itself bears witness with our spirit that we are children of God, ¹⁷and if children, then heirs, heirs of God and joint heirs with Christ, if only we suffer with him so that we may also be glorified with him.

Destiny of Glory. ¹⁸I consider that the sufferings of this present time are as nothing compared with the glory to be revealed for us. ¹⁹For creation awaits with eager expectation the revelation of the children of God; ²⁰for creation was made subject to futility, not of its own accord but because of the one who subjected it, in hope ²¹that creation itself would be set free from slavery to corruption and share in the glorious freedom of the children of God. ²²We know that all creation is groaning in labor pains even until now; ²³and not only that, but we ourselves, who have the firstfruits of the Spirit, we also groan within ourselves as we wait for adoption, the redemption of our bodies. ²⁴For in hope we were saved. Now hope that sees for itself is not hope. For who hopes for what one sees? ²⁵But if we hope for what we do not see, we wait with endurance.

---

is talking about eschatology in the process of realization. Scholars who pursue a story approach to Romans rightly note that Paul seems to momentarily draw the curtain back from the end time to show believers what it will be like. At the same time, Paul stresses that believers are already experiencing in the Spirit, in hope, what God's gracious purpose has in store for them. They have been saved—in hope (8:24). I also invite my readers to see how often Paul joins hands with the experience of the Gentile believers in Romans by frequently using "we." I refer to 8:16, 17, 18, 22, 23, 24, 25, 26, 28.

Here are the believers' present experiences that point to the future. They are "children of God," sons and daughters of God, brothers and sisters of Jesus. Romans 8:15 says pointedly: "*You* received a spirit of adoption, through which *we* cry, *Abba*, 'Father'" (emphasis added to "you" and "we"). The Holy Spirit has brought about this experience of adoption into God's family (see 8:16). Amidst present sufferings, glory awaits believers. That is their hope, for they are not like the pagans, "who have no hope" (1 Thess 4:13). They await what Revelation 21:1 refers to as " a new heaven and a new earth," that is, a time when God's curse upon humanity and the earth is lifted. See Genesis 3:17-19: "Cursed be the ground because of you! / In toil shall you eat its yield / all the days of your life. / Thorns and thistles shall it bring forth to you. . . . / By the sweat of your face / shall you get bread to eat." Believers await in groaning the fulfillment of the firstfruits of the Spirit, namely, the redemption of their entire selves (8:23).

²⁶In the same way, the Spirit too comes to the aid of our weakness; for we do not know how to pray as we ought, but the Spirit itself intercedes with inexpressible groanings. ²⁷And the one who searches hearts knows what is the intention of the Spirit, because it intercedes for the holy ones according to God's will.

God's Indomitable Love in Christ. ²⁸We know that all things work for good for those who love God, who are called according to his purpose. ²⁹For those he foreknew he also predestined to be conformed to the image of his Son, so that he might be the firstborn among many brothers. ³⁰And those he predestined he also called; and those he called he also justified; and those he justified he also glorified.

³¹What then shall we say to this? If God is for us, who can be against us? ³²He who did not spare his own Son but handed him over for us all, how will he not also give us everything else along with him? ³³Who will bring a charge

---

Among the vicissitudes of human life and the life of faith, the Spirit comes to believers' aid and intercedes with God for them. As James D. G. Dunn says so well: "The Spirit is seen here as typically active not so much in the heights of spiritual rapture as in the depths of human inability to cope." In 8:28-30 Paul captures the final experience believers have: It is the confidence born of their faith "that all things work for good for those who love God" (8:28). Glorification is the ultimate destiny of all who have faith in Jesus Christ as their Lord (8:30). Paul speaks of it as already present.

8:31-39 A hymn to the God who is for us

I have counted a dozen occurrences of "we/our/us" in the Greek of this relatively short passage. Paul again engages in *pathos* and identifies himself with his listeners. To what does "this" in 8:31 refer? Is it a reference to the sufferings Paul mentions in 8:18-25? I would suggest that it's a reference to the various battles which believers wage against the powers of sin, death, and the flesh and which Paul has treated in Romans 5:11–8:30.

Paul once again adopts the style of a scholastic diatribe and raises questions in 8:31, 32, 33, 34, 35. The scene is the courtroom of the Last Judgment. Paul's answers seem like an early creed and reveal deep faith in what God has done for believers: God is for us; God lovingly handed his Son over for our salvation; God acquits the ungodly; Christ Jesus died, was raised, is at the right hand of the Father, and intercedes for us; we conquer overwhelmingly through the God who loves us; God loves us in Christ Jesus our Lord. The trials that Paul experienced as a missionary and apostle do not have the power to separate him from the love of Christ (8:35). It is for God's sake that Paul endures all this, as he demonstrates

SCRIPTURE GROUP

BARCLAY, ANNA MAY	6 GREENWOOD DR.	439 5530
BARDWELL, MARY	79 FERNBANK AVE.	439 5907
COML, SARAH	70 CAMBRIDGE	439 2716
DAVITT, MARY	39 HUNTERSFIELD	439 6018
DEXTER, TERESA	11 PINETREE DR.	439 5876
FINAN, STELLA	402 ELKIN CT.	475 9818
GILDAY, MARGARET	30 CHARLES BLVD.	439 5502
HOUCK, MICHELINE	8 SLINGERLANDS DR.	768 2162
KERRIGAN, BETTE		439 2464
LEAVITT, JEAN	77 FERNBANK AVE.	439 6960
LYNCH, MARGE	45 CONSTITUTION	439 5509
RIGHTMEYER, NOREEN	61 BEACON	439 5343
SLOANE, MAGDELENA	5 MERCIFIELD PL.	439 8350
WELCH, MURIEL	48 CARSTEAD	439 3123

against God's chosen ones? It is God who acquits us. [34]Who will condemn? It is Christ [Jesus] who died, rather, was raised, who also is at the right hand of God, who indeed intercedes for us. [35]What will separate us from the love of Christ? Will anguish, or distress, or persecution, or famine, or nakedness, or peril, or the sword? [36]As it is written:

"For your sake we are being slain all the day;
we are looked upon as sheep to be slaughtered."

[37]No, in all these things we conquer overwhelmingly through him who loved us. [38]For I am convinced that neither death, nor life, nor angels, nor principalities, nor present things, nor future things, nor powers, [39]nor height, nor depth, nor any other creature will be able to separate us from the love of God in Christ Jesus our Lord.

V. Jews and Gentiles in God's Plan

9 **Paul's Love for Israel.** [1]I speak the truth in Christ, I do not lie; my conscience joins with the holy Spirit in bearing me witness [2]that I have great sorrow and constant anguish in my heart. [3]For I could wish that I myself were accursed and separated from

---

from Psalm 43:23 in the Septuagint. No creature whatsoever, no matter how fearsome, is able to separate believers from God's love, manifested in Christ Jesus our Lord (8:38-39).

This hymn has provided courage to believers after national, community, and personal disasters. People battling cancer have drawn tremendous strength by looking at God through the lens of this hymn. Believers of all stripes rejoice that Paul shared his experience of God, which forms the basis for our experience of God.

JEWS AND GENTILES IN GOD'S PLAN

Romans 9:1–11:36

9:1-5 Paul's *ethos, pathos,* and logic on dress parade in the service of theodicy

I make four opening remarks for all of Romans 9–11. The rousing hymn in praise of God that Paul created in Romans 8:31-39 almost seems to defy any new thoughts. Shouldn't Paul conclude his letter, send greetings, and call it quits? If Paul were only dealing with the salvation of humankind, he might very well stop with 8:39. But in Romans Paul is concerned with God and how justification by faith for both Gentiles and Jews accords with God's earlier choice of Israel as God's special people. Remember that the theme sentence of Romans goes: The gospel "is the power of God for the salvation of everyone who believes: for *Jew first*, and then Greek" (1:16; emphasis added).

Christ for the sake of my brothers, my kin according to the flesh. [4]They are Israelites; theirs the adoption, the glory, the covenants, the giving of the law, the worship, and the promises; [5]theirs the patriarchs, and from them, according to the flesh, is the Messiah. God who is over all be blessed forever. Amen.

God's Free Choice. [6]But it is not that the word of God has failed. For not all who are of Israel are Israel, [7]nor are they all children of Abraham because they are his descendants; but "It is through Isaac that descendants shall bear your name." [8]This means that it is not the children of the flesh who are the

---

Second, Paul, a fervent Jew, the apostle to the Gentiles, bares his heart (*pathos* and *ethos*) on the question: Has the word of God failed? (9:6). Twenty-seven times, compared with eight in Romans 1:18–8:39, Paul uses "I." Stanley Stowers captures Paul's *pathos* and *ethos* well: "Even his mission to the Gentiles turns out to be an episode in the self-story of an Israelite acting for the sake of his people."

Third, the *logic* of Paul's argument in these three chapters is thoroughly scriptural—almost 40 percent of these ninety verses. James W. Aageson has well said: "The reliability of *God's word* to Israel was at stake; and it was to *God's word*, the Scriptures, that Paul turned to argue that it had not failed." In my commentary I will be tracking Paul's use of Scripture and implore my readers to be patient as they gradually discern how Paul is joining Scripture texts via themes. At the same time I advise my readers that Paul, even in Romans 9–11, does not neglect scholastic diatribe, for example, Romans 11:17-24.

Finally, although Paul is truly a religious genius, it is difficult to imagine him composing Romans 9–11 off the top of his head. Paul has frequently wrestled with and anguished over the issues of these chapters and may have preached a sermon or two about them.

In 9:1-5 Paul engages in deep and sincere *pathos* ("great sorrow and constant anguish") over his fellow Jews, the majority of whom have not believed in the gospel of Jesus as Messiah and Lord. God has gifted them so generously. While nothing can separate believers from the love of Christ (8:35), Paul, similar to Moses in Exodus 32:32, is willing to be "separated from Christ for the sake of" his brothers and sisters, his kin according to the flesh.

9:6-13 Paul's thesis and scriptural arguments from the patriarchs

In 9:6 Paul states the proposition that he will be defending from God's word throughout Romans 9–11: The word of God has not failed. The word of God's promise (9:9) and God's call (9:7, 12) are determinative of who

children of God, but the children of the promise are counted as descendants. [9]For this is the wording of the promise, "About this time I shall return and Sarah will have a son." [10]And not only that, but also when Rebecca had conceived children by one husband, our father Isaac—[11]before they had yet been born or had done anything, good or bad, in order that God's elective plan might continue, [12]not by works but by his call—she was told, "The older shall serve the younger." [13]As it is written:

> "I loved Jacob
> but hated Esau."

[14]What then are we to say? Is there injustice on the part of God? Of course not! [15]For he says to Moses:

> "I will show mercy to whom I will,
> I will take pity on whom I will."

God's children are. For example, "This means that it is not the children of the flesh who are the children of God, but the children of the promise are counted as descendants" (9:8). Paul's Scripture quotations come from Genesis 21:12; 18:10, 14; 25:23, the earliest narratives of God's people. Even the citation from a prophetic text (Mal 1:2-3 in Rom 9:13) refers back to the very beginnings of Israel. In this first section of Scripture argumentation, Paul has introduced in 9:7b and 12 a theme that he will pick up in Romans 9:24-26, namely, the theme of "call." The citation from Genesis 21:12 in Romans 9:7b should be translated: "In Isaac your offspring will be called."

9:14-18 God is not unjust; God is sovereign

After using elements of scholastic diatribe throughout Romans 1–8, Paul does not think it time to put it to bed. It has been so useful in helping him engage his listeners. Although God has chosen one and not another, God surely is not unjust. In Romans 9:15 Paul proves God's sovereignty by quoting Exodus 33:19 exactly as it is in the Septuagint: "I will show mercy to whom I will. I will take pity on whom I will" (author's translation).

In 9:16 Paul draws his conclusion by picking up the theme of God's mercy: "So it depends not upon a person's will or exertion, but upon God, who shows mercy." Paul's quotation from Exodus 9:16 is almost verbatim as it describes God's power over Pharaoh. Using the same inferential words he did in 9:16 *(ara oun)*, Paul draws his conclusion in 9:18, again emphasizing God's mercy: "Consequently, he has mercy upon whom he wills, and he hardens whom he wills." Having employed the theme of God's call in 9:6-13, Paul now joins it to the theme of God's mercy: God is the one who calls in God's mercy. The astute reader will notice that Paul is joining Scripture quotations together by means of identical words and themes.

[16]So it depends not upon a person's will or exertion, but upon God, who shows mercy. [17]For the scripture says to Pharaoh, "This is why I have raised you up, to show my power through you that my name may be proclaimed throughout the earth." [18]Consequently, he has mercy upon whom he wills, and he hardens whom he wills.

[19]You will say to me then, "Why [then] does he still find fault? For who can oppose his will?" [20]But who indeed are you, a human being, to talk back to God? Will what is made say to its maker, "Why have you created me so?" [21]Or does not the potter have a right over the clay, to make out of the same lump one vessel for a noble purpose and another for an ignoble one? [22]What if God, wishing to show his wrath and make known his power, has endured with much patience the vessels of wrath made for destruction? [23]This was to make known the riches of his glory to the vessels of mercy, which he has prepared previously for glory, [24]namely, us whom he has called, not only from the Jews but also from the Gentiles.

Witness of the Prophets. [25]As indeed he says in Hosea:

"Those who were not my people
   I will call 'my people,'
and her who was not beloved
   I will call 'beloved.'
[26]And in the very place where it
   was said to them, 'You are
   not my people,'
there they shall be called children
   of the living God."

[27]And Isaiah cries out concerning Israel, "Though the number of the Israelites were like the sand of the sea, only a remnant will be saved; [28]for decisively and quickly will the Lord execute sentence upon the earth." [29]And as Isaiah predicted:

"Unless the Lord of hosts had left
   us descendants,
we would have become like
   Sodom
and have been made like
   Gomorrah."

9:19-29 God's mercy, call, and ultimate fidelity

The questions/objections of scholastic diatribe hold 9:19-22 together. Paul combines citations from Isaiah 29:16 and Job 9:12 to answer these objections. How dare a human being even raise such objections! In 9:23 Paul resumes his theme of "mercy" and in 9:25-26 his theme of "call" to show that not only Jews but also Gentiles receive mercy and are called. But God has foreseen through Isaiah that not all is lost for Israel, which has not responded positively to the gospel. Quoting Isaiah 10:22, Paul says: "'Although the number of the Israelites were like the sand of the sea, a remnant will be saved'" (author's translation). The theme of "remnant," introduced here, will reappear in Romans 11:5. Key, too, are words from Isaiah 1:9 in Romans 9:29: The Lord has left us descendants (literally: "a seed").

Righteousness Based on Faith. [30]What then shall we say? That Gentiles, who did not pursue righteousness, have achieved it, that is, righteousness that comes from faith; [31]but that Israel, who pursued the law of righteousness, did not attain to that law? [32]Why not? Because they did it not by faith, but as if it could be done by works. They stumbled over the stone that causes stumbling, [33]as it is written:

"Behold, I am laying a stone in Zion
　that will make people stumble
　and a rock that will make them
　　fall,
and whoever believes in him shall
　not be put to shame."

[10] [1]Brothers, my heart's desire and prayer to God on their behalf is for salvation. [2]I testify with regard to them that they have zeal for God, but it is not discerning. [3]For, in their

9:30-33 Surprisingly pagans have faith; unfortunately Israel has not

Paul moves his considerations along by two more questions in 9:30 and 32 and by adding in 9:31-32 the way God has chosen both Jews and Gentiles, that is, through faith and not by works. Paul buttresses his considerations with a combined citation from two passages in Isaiah where he finds the same words. The words "whoever *believes* in him shall not be put to shame" come from Isaiah 28:16, which also contains the word "stone" (emphasis added). Isaiah 8:14 in the Septuagint also contains the word "stone" as well as "stumble" and "rock." Paul's interpretation of these two passages is daring and christological, for the stone laid by God in Zion as a sure foundation has become the stumbling stone, Jesus Christ. See 1 Peter 2:6-8 for a similar use of Isaiah 28:16 and 8:14.

10:1-13 Righteousness through faith

Romans 10:1-4 continues Paul's discussion of righteousness, and 10:5-13 provides scriptural support. Paul's concern for his fellow Jews is palpable (10:1). He does not slander them, for they manifest zeal for worshiping God and obeying God's law that is genuine (10:2). See, for example, 1 Maccabees 2:27: "Then Mattathias went through the city shouting, 'Let everyone who is zealous for the law and who stands by the covenant follow after me.'" But they have not submitted to the righteousness of God that has been revealed in Christ Jesus and in the gospel. Through Jesus Christ God has acquitted believers. What the law tried to accomplish, God has accomplished in Jesus Christ. Thus he is the end and goal of the law.

The Scripture citation of Leviticus 18:5 in Romans 10:5 is verbatim and supports the view that righteousness comes from the law. Paul's Scripture citations in Romans 10:6-8 stem from Deuteronomy 9:4; 30:12-14, and Psalm 106:26 in the Septuagint. Although the passages from Deuteronomy talk

unawareness of the righteousness that comes from God and their attempt to establish their own [righteousness], they did not submit to the righteousness of God. ⁴For Christ is the end of the law for the justification of everyone who has faith.

⁵Moses writes about the righteousness that comes from [the] law, "The one who does these things will live by them." ⁶But the righteousness that comes from faith says, "Do not say in your heart, 'Who will go up into heaven?' (that is, to bring Christ down) ⁷or 'Who will go down into the abyss?' (that is, to bring Christ up from the dead)." ⁸But what does it say?

"The word is near you,
    in your mouth and in your heart"

(that is, the word of faith that we preach), ⁹for, if you confess with your mouth that Jesus is Lord and believe in your heart that God raised him from the dead, you will be saved. ¹⁰For one believes with the heart and so is justified, and one confesses with the mouth and so is saved. ¹¹For the scripture says, "No one who believes in him will be put to shame." ¹²For there is no distinction between Jew and Greek; the same Lord is Lord of all, enriching all who call upon him. ¹³For "everyone who calls on the name of the Lord will be saved."

¹⁴But how can they call on him in whom they have not believed? And how can they believe in him of whom they have not heard? And how can

about God's gift of the law, Paul has interpreted them christologically via his "that is" clauses in 10:6-8.

Paul's main point about the righteousness that comes from faith is evidenced in his explicit quotation of Deuteronomy 30:14 in Romans 10:8: "'The word is near you, / in your mouth and in your heart' / (that is, the word of faith that we preach)." In Romans 10:9 Paul interprets "mouth" from Deuteronomy 30:14, and in 10:10 he explains "heart" from Deuteronomy 30:14 and does so by relying upon early confessions of faith: Jesus is Lord; God raised Jesus from the dead. In 10:11 Paul recycles and universalizes the quotation from Isaiah 28:16 he quoted earlier in 9:33. Paul's final citation in this section is verbatim from Joel 3:5. It is God who is described as calling in Romans 9:7, 12, 24, 25, 26. Now Gentile and Jewish believers do the calling.

10:14-21 God's chosen people have been disobedient while the senseless Gentiles have believed

This section shows that God's chosen people have no excuse for not believing the gospel. As is his custom, Paul makes his case by means of the questions of scholastic diatribe and his responses, which are largely taken from Scripture, especially Isaiah. One theme that joins this passage

they hear without someone to preach? [15]And how can people preach unless they are sent? As it is written, "How beautiful are the feet of those who bring [the] good news!" [16]But not everyone has heeded the good news; for Isaiah says, "Lord, who has believed what was heard from us?" [17]Thus faith comes from what is heard, and what is heard comes through the word of Christ. [18]But I ask, did they not hear? Certainly they did; for

> "Their voice has gone forth to all
> the earth,
> and their words to the ends of
> the world."

[19]But I ask, did not Israel understand? First Moses says:

> "I will make you jealous of those
> who are not a nation;
> with a senseless nation I will
> make you angry."

[20]Then Isaiah speaks boldly and says:

> "I was found [by] those who were
> not seeking me;
> I revealed myself to those who
> were not asking for me."

[21]But regarding Israel he says, "All day long I stretched out my hands to a disobedient and contentious people."

11 **The Remnant of Israel.** [1]I ask, then, has God rejected his people? Of course not! For I too am an Israelite, a descendant of Abraham, of the tribe of Benjamin. [2]God has not rejected his people whom he foreknew. Do you not

---

to the previous section is that of *word*. See 10:8: "'The word is near you, / in your mouth and in your heart' / (that is, the word of faith that we preach)." See also 10:17: "and what is heard comes through the word of Christ," and 10:18: "and their words to the end of the world." While Paul underscores the belief of the foolish Gentiles (10:19-20) and chastises Israel's disobedience (10:21), he announces in advance his "solution" to the nonbelief of God's chosen people. Quoting Deuteronomy 32:21, Paul says: "I will make you jealous of those who are not a nation" (Rom 10:19). See Romans 11:11-15 for Paul's treatment of this theme of jealousy.

11:1-10 Israel's rejection is partial

By means of diatribal questions and quotations from Scripture, Paul continues to present his resolution of the place in God's plan of Israel's failure to believe in Jesus Christ. Paul's own experience as a Jew who is a Christian (11:2) answers the first question (11:1). Paul cites the example of the seven thousand who remained faithful during Elijah's time as further proof. Just above the verbs "I alone *am left*" (11:3) and "I *have left* for myself" (11:4) hovers the theme that Paul introduced earlier in Romans 9:27—the remnant (emphasis added). In 11:5 Paul makes the connection explicit: "So also at the present time there is a remnant, chosen by grace."

know what the scripture says about Elijah, how he pleads with God against Israel? ³"Lord, they have killed your prophets, they have torn down your altars, and I alone am left, and they are seeking my life." ⁴But what is God's response to him? "I have left for myself seven thousand men who have not knelt to Baal." ⁵So also at the present time there is a remnant, chosen by grace. ⁶But if by grace, it is no longer because of works; otherwise grace would no longer be grace. ⁷What then? What Israel was seeking it did not attain, but the elect attained it; the rest were hardened, ⁸as it is written:

"God gave them a spirit of deep sleep,
    eyes that should not see
    and ears that should not hear,
down to this very day."

⁹And David says:

"Let their table become a snare and
    a trap,
    a stumbling block and a retribu-
        tion for them;
¹⁰let their eyes grow dim so that
        they may not see,
    and keep their backs bent
        forever."

The Gentiles' Salvation. ¹¹Hence I ask, did they stumble so as to fall? Of course not! But through their transgression salvation has come to the Gentiles, so as to make them jealous. ¹²Now if their ▶ transgression is enrichment for the world, and if their diminished number is enrichment for the Gentiles, how much more their full number.

¹³Now I am speaking to you Gen- ▶ tiles. Inasmuch then as I am the apostle to the Gentiles, I glory in my ministry ¹⁴in order to make my race jealous and thus save some of them. ¹⁵For if their ▶ rejection is the reconciliation of the

---

Paul concludes this section by referring to the Law (Deut 29:3), the Prophets (Isa 29:10), and the Writings (Ps 68:24 in the Septuagint) and links all three by the catchword "eyes." James D. G. Dunn helpfully maintains that the adverbial phrase *dia pantos*, with which Paul concludes this section, "is better translated 'continually' than 'for ever.'" The very existence of a remnant indicates that the rejection is only partial.

11:11-24 Paul censures Gentile Christian arrogance

Paul's main point about the destiny of God's chosen people comes across loud and clear: God has not abandoned them. See, for example, 11:24: "how much more will they who belong to it by nature be grafted back into their own olive tree." In making this point, Paul addresses his Gentile listeners and censures them for possible arrogance against unbelieving Israel.

Readers who have been diligently tracking Paul's use of Scripture quotations in Romans 9–11 may have had the same experience I did, that is, the realization that Paul does not cite a single word of Scripture in this

world, what will their acceptance be but life from the dead? ¹⁶If the firstfruits are holy, so is the whole batch of dough; and if the root is holy, so are the branches.

¹⁷But if some of the branches were broken off, and you, a wild olive shoot, were grafted in their place and have come to share in the rich root of the olive tree, ¹⁸do not boast against the branches. If you do boast, consider that you do not support the root; the root supports you. ¹⁹Indeed you will say, "Branches were broken off so that I might be grafted in." ²⁰That is so. They were broken off because of unbelief, but you are there because of faith. So do not become haughty, but stand in awe. ²¹For if God did not spare the natural branches, [perhaps] he will not spare you either. ²²See, then, the kind-

ness and severity of God: severity toward those who fell, but God's kindness to you, provided you remain in his kindness; otherwise you too will be cut off. ²³And they also, if they do not remain in unbelief, will be grafted in, for God is able to graft them in again. ²⁴For if you were cut from what is by nature a wild olive tree, and grafted, contrary to nature, into a cultivated one, how much more will they who belong to it by nature be grafted back into their own olive tree.

God's Irrevocable Call. ²⁵I do not want you to be unaware of this mystery, brothers, so that you will not become wise [in] your own estimation: a hardening has come upon Israel in part, until the full number of the Gentiles comes in, ²⁶and thus all Israel will be saved, as it is written:

section. Rather, elements from scholastic diatribe dominate this passage, for example, 11:11 and 11:17-24. In 11:13-16 Paul addressed the Gentile Christians in the second person plural. In 11:17 he begins to use the second person singular in his personification of the wild olive shoot and in doing so hones in on possible boasting and arrogant taunting on the part of Gentile Christians. Note how Paul singles out the imaginary person in 11:17 by using "you." Romans 11:18 continues to address the imaginary person with imperatives. Verses 19-24 formulate a dialogue between Paul and his imaginary person. Of course, Paul's responses and imperatives carry the day.

11:25-32 God has mercy on all

Paul's Scripture citation in Romans 11:26-27 is a combination of Isaiah 59:20-21 and Isaiah 27:9. Most important is Paul's modification of Isaiah 59:20, where the Greek of the Septuagint reads *heneken* ("for the sake of"), that is, "The deliverer will come for the sake of Zion" (author's translation). By exchanging *ek* ("out of") for *heneken*, Paul makes a potent christological statement: Christ is the deliverer and has come from Zion (and indeed for Zion's sake).

"The deliverer will come out of Zion,
  he will turn away godlessness
    from Jacob;
[27]and this is my covenant with them
  when I take away their sins."

[28]In respect to the gospel, they are enemies on your account; but in respect to election, they are beloved because of the patriarchs. [29]For the gifts and the call of God are irrevocable.

Triumph of God's Mercy. [30]Just as you once disobeyed God but have now received mercy because of their disobedience, [31]so they have now disobeyed in order that, by virtue of the mercy shown to you, they too may [now] receive mercy. [32]For God delivered all to disobedience, that he might have mercy upon all.

[33]Oh, the depth of the riches and wisdom and knowledge of God! How inscrutable are his judgments and how unsearchable his ways!

[34]"For who has known the mind of
    the Lord
  or who has been his counselor?"
[35]"Or who has given him anything
    that he may be repaid?"

[36]For from him and through him and for him are all things. To him be glory forever. Amen.

Throughout this section, which has Gentile believers in mind, there is an ebb and flow between universality and particularity. Three statements point to universality: "the full number of the Gentiles" (11:25), "thus all Israel will be saved" (11:26), and "that he might have mercy upon all" (11:32). Romans 11:29 breathes particularity: "For the gifts and the call of God are irrevocable." How God holds together universality and particularity is being revealed now as God lets men and women in on his mystery, and we frail human beings struggle mightily and sometimes sin grievously in our attempts to fathom and live by this mystery.

11:33-36 Praise to God

Paul's Scripture citation in Romans 11:34 is verbatim from Isaiah 40:13. Scholars are unsure to what extent Paul cites Scripture and what Scripture he cites in Romans 11:35. Job 41:3 has been proposed. These verses are justifiably called hymnic. In Greek the rhyme of 11:33 sounds forth: *ploutou, theou, autou, autou, anex-, anex-.* The rhythmic driving force of 11:36 even roars through the English: "From him and through him and for him are all things." Paul's use of quotations from Scripture and rhyme and rhythm serve one purpose: the praise of God, whose ways he has been describing since Romans 1:16. Human beings stand in awe and in worship of this gracious and merciful God.

VI. The Duties of Christians

12 **Sacrifice of Body and Mind.** [1]I urge you therefore, brothers, by the mercies of God, to offer your bodies as a living sacrifice, holy and pleasing to God, your spiritual worship. [2]Do not conform yourselves to this age but be transformed by the renewal of your

THE DUTIES OF CHRISTIANS

Romans 12:1–15:13

12:1-3 The overture to Paul's exhortations

I offer three preliminary considerations for all of Romans 12:1–15:13. First, those of us who have been paying close attention to Paul's use of pronouns will notice how frequently he employs imperatives in Romans 12:1–15:13. For example, 12:2: "Do not conform yourself to this age," and 15:2: "Let each of us please our neighbor for the good, for building up."

Second, I supply some background material so that we may be better able to recognize the similarities and differences between the block of exhortations in 12:1–15:13 and those in other writings. The exhortations that Paul artistically presents in 12:9-21 have some parallels in Jesus' Sermon on the Mount. Compare Matthew 5:44: "Love your enemies, and pray for those who persecute you," and Romans 12:14: "Bless those who persecute [you], bless and do not curse them."

An example of a very common "two ways teaching" is found in a section of the *Didache*, which dates to the same time as Romans. The *Didache* reads:

> There are two ways, one of life and one of death, and the difference between the two ways is great. This then is the way of life. First, love the God who made you, and second, your neighbor as yourself. And whatever you do not want to happen to you, do not do to another. . . . And now the second commandment of the teaching. Do not murder, do not commit adultery, do not engage in pederasty, do not engage in sexual immorality. Do not steal, do not practice magic, do not use enchanted potions, do not abort a fetus or kill a child that is born (1:1-2 and 2:1-2; Loeb translation modified).

The *Didache* continues:

> And the way of death is this. First of all it is evil and filled with a curse: murders, adulteries, passions, sexual immoralities, robberies . . . deceit, arrogance, malice, insolence. . . . It is filled with persecutors of the good, haters of the truth. . . . Murderers of children and

81

mind, that you may discern what is the will of God, what is good and pleasing and perfect.

Many Parts in One Body. ³For by the grace given to me I tell everyone among you not to think of himself more highly than one ought to think, but to think soberly, each according to the measure of faith that God has apportioned. ⁴For as in one body we have ▶

---

corruptors of what God has fashioned, who turn their backs on the needy, oppress the afflicted, and support the wealthy (5:1-2; Loeb modified).

Although Paul has some items in common with the "two ways teaching," he did not see fit to adopt this very popular "ethical" schema.

Third, one of the reasons Paul does not adopt such traditional materials as the "two ways teaching" is that he is spelling out the practical implications of his theology of love (12:9-21; 13:8-10; 14:1–15:13) and the Spirit (12:4-8) and of faith (12:3, 6; 14:1, 22-23). In brief, he is telling the Romans in 12:1–15:13 what Romans 5:5 means: "the love of God has been poured out into our hearts through the holy Spirit that has been given to us."

I make three points about Romans 12:1-3. First, 12:1-3 and what follows are not independent of what has gone before in the previous eleven chapters. Paul uses his authority (his *ethos*) and draws inferences ("therefore") from what he has previously stated and now summarizes in the phrase "by the mercies of God."

Second, there is a very close connection between what Paul says in 12:1 ("offer your bodies as a living sacrifice") and what he had said earlier, for instance, in 1:24: "Therefore, God handed them over to impurity through the lusts of their hearts for the mutual degradation of their bodies." Paul's Gentile listeners are now worshiping God (12:1) rather than creatures (1:25).

Third, behind the command "Do not conform yourself to this age" (12:2) stands the eschatological perspective that has dominated Romans 1–11; for example, 3:21: "But *now* the righteousness of God has been manifested" (emphasis added). The eschatological dimension of 12:2 also points ahead to 13:11-14, which deals with the perspective of the end time and rounds off this section of exhortations. Technically, 12:2 and 13:11-14 form a thematic *inclusio*, that is, the placement of similar material at the beginning and end of a section.

12:4-8 One body with many gifts

In 1 Corinthians 12–14 Paul wrote a far more extensive treatment of the one body with many parts and of the gifts *(charismata)* of the Holy

The Appian Way, the oldest and most famous road built by the ancient Romans, was begun in 312 B.C. and was later extended to Brindisi, where ships to Greece could be boarded.

many parts, and all the parts do not have the same function, ⁵so we, though many, are one body in Christ and individually parts of one another. ⁶Since we have gifts that differ according to the grace given to us, let us exercise them: if prophecy, in proportion to the faith; ⁷if ministry, in ministering; if one is a teacher, in teaching; ⁸if one exhorts, in exhortation; if one contributes, in generosity; if one is over others, with diligence; if one does acts of mercy, with cheerfulness.

Mutual Love. ⁹Let love be sincere; hate what is evil, hold on to what is good; ¹⁰love one another with mutual affection; anticipate one another in showing honor. ¹¹Do not grow slack in zeal, be fervent in spirit, serve the Lord. ¹²Rejoice in hope, endure in affliction,

---

Spirit. Although here in Romans 12:4-8 Paul does not say that the "gifts" (12:6) come from the Holy Spirit, expressions such as "according to the grace given us" seem to presuppose the Holy Spirit (12:6). "Prophecy in proportion to the faith" (12:6) invites special comment. Prophecy is not so much foretelling the future but forthtelling, and could very well blend with the gift of exhortation (12:8).

"In proportion to the faith" is a phrase that resonates in Christian communities across the ages. One believer looking at a text of Scripture may see a valid but surface meaning, whereas the prophet may see far deeper and speak more challengingly about the same Scripture text. The development of Paul's thought in 1 Corinthians 12–14 may also give us a clue as to why Paul in Romans 12:9-21 gives exhortations about love. Paul's hymn to love in 1 Corinthians 13 occurs after a detailed discussion of the body of Christ and the gifts of the Spirit. The Corinthians are to pursue love in exercising their gifts (1 Cor 14:1).

12:9-21 The path of love

It is certainly easier to delve into the literary structure and theology of this passage than to abide by its thirty injunctions. Yes, thirty. That's what Philip F. Esler maintains. I just counted them, and he's right. For example, 12:11 has three: "Do not grow slack in zeal, be fervent in spirit, serve the Lord"; 12:16 has four: "Have the same regard for one another; do not be haughty but associate with the lowly; do not be wise in your own estimation."

With its flowing translation, the NAB translation of 12:16 hides some of its artistry. Here Paul uses the same Greek verb *(phronein)* three times ("have the same regard; do not be haughty; do not be wise"). Paul's artistry also shines forth in the connection between 12:13-14, where the same Greek verb *(diokein)* occurs and stands behind *"exercise* hospitality" and

persevere in prayer. [13]Contribute to the needs of the holy ones, exercise hospitality. [14]Bless those who persecute [you], bless and do not curse them. [15]Rejoice with those who rejoice, weep with those who weep. [16]Have the same regard for one another; do not be haughty but associate with the lowly; do not be wise in your own estimation. [17]Do not repay anyone evil for evil; be concerned for what is noble in the sight of all. [18]If possible, on your part, live at peace with all. [19]Beloved, do not look for revenge but leave room for the wrath; for it is written, "Vengeance is mine, I will repay, says the Lord." [20]Rather, "if your enemy is hungry, feed him; if he is thirsty, give him something to drink; for by so doing you will heap burning coals upon his head." [21]Do not be conquered by evil but conquer evil with good.

13 **Obedience to Authority.** [1]Let every person be subordinate to the higher authorities, for there is no authority except from God, and those

---

"bless those who *persecute*" (emphasis added). Paul's sprinkling of similar mnemonic devices throughout 12:9-16 has led Esler to suggest that we have here "a precious fragment of Paul's oral proclamation on the subject of the love that must characterize the life and identity of Christ-followers."

The injunctions of Romans 12:17-21 deal with peace, forgiveness, and non-retaliation. They are different, too, in that they contain the only explicit citations of Scripture in this section: Deuteronomy 32:35 in Romans 12:19 and Proverbs 25:21-22 in Romans 12:20. Giving food and drink to an enemy (12:19) has the result of heaping "burning coals upon his head" (12:20). Obviously, we are not to take "heaping burning coals upon" someone's head literally. I rely on Frederick W. Danker's interpretation of this obscure action: to "cause a person to blush with shame and remorse." In our language, especially in certain regions, there are expressions that are opaque to outsiders. For example, the first time I heard "The pastor threw a ram," I had little idea what it meant and tried to visualize an elderly pastor throwing cattle around. I was told that the pastor was very angry. I had to convert "ram" into an expression for "anger." Similarly, we have to convert "heaping burning coals upon" into an expression for "shaming a person."

Some years ago my work took me to a diocese where the Scripture adopted for reflection and implementation for the entire year was Romans 12:9-21. What a whale of an agenda for any church, local or diocesan!

13:1-7 Civil authority and the believer

Why does Paul say what he does in this passage and why now? The answer to "why now" is easier to provide. In this section Paul is tidying

that exist have been established by God. ²Therefore, whoever resists authority opposes what God has appointed, and those who oppose it will bring judgment upon themselves. ³For rulers are not a cause of fear to good conduct, but to evil. Do you wish to have no fear of authority? Then do what is good and you will receive approval from it, ⁴for it is a servant of God for your good. But if you do evil, be afraid, for it does not bear the sword without purpose; it is the servant of God to inflict wrath on the evildoer. ⁵Therefore, it is necessary to be subject not only because of the wrath but also because of conscience. ⁶This is why you also pay taxes, for the authorities are ministers of God, devoting themselves to this very thing. ⁷Pay to all their dues, taxes to whom taxes are due, toll to whom toll is due, respect to whom respect is due, honor to whom honor is due.

Love Fulfills the Law. ⁸Owe nothing to anyone, except to love one another; for the one who loves another

---

up some loose ends from what he has just said in 12:17-21. If Christians are not to exact revenge for evil done them (12:19), who is? They are to leave "room for the wrath" (12:19), which God will exercise through legitimate civil authority. See how "wrath" recurs in 13:4-5, for example, 13:4: "It is the servant of God to inflict wrath on the evildoer." Paul is also providing some extra specificity to what he said in 12:9: "Hold on to what is good." Notice that the word "good" occurs three times in 13:3-4 in verses couched in the diatribal "you" singular style. For instance, 13:3: "Then do what is good and you will receive approval from it."

Paul was raised in a hierarchical and patriarchal society and was heir to views of the role of government in God's created order. In its address to kings and magistrates, Wisdom 6:3 expresses something very similar to what Paul says in Romans 13:1: "Because authority was given you by the LORD and sovereignty by the Most High." But Wisdom 6:3 immediately characterizes God as the One "who shall probe your works and scrutinize your counsels!"

Paul does not give absolute authority to the Roman emperors who ruled the roost in his day. Such rulers are "servant[s] of God" (13:4), not gods to be worshiped. Luke Timothy Johnson has expressed well the hermeneutical implications of 13:1-7: "If all civil authority is from God and ordered under God, then it equally follows that a civil authority that does not respond to God's will can be considered disqualified as a true authority, and so could be resisted 'for conscience's sake.'"

13:8-10 Love your neighbor as yourself

Paul continues what has been called his "general exhortations" by double linking Romans 13:8-10 to what has gone before. The immediate

has fulfilled the law. ⁹The commandments, "You shall not commit adultery;
you shall not kill; you shall not steal;
you shall not covet," and whatever
other commandment there may be, are
summed up in this saying, [namely]
"You shall love your neighbor as yourself." ¹⁰Love does no evil to the neighbor;
hence, love is the fulfillment of the law.

Awareness of the End of Time.
¹¹And do this because you know the
time; it is the hour now for you to awake
from sleep. For our salvation is nearer
now than when we first believed; ¹²the
night is advanced, the day is at hand.
Let us then throw off the works of darkness [and] put on the armor of light;
¹³let us conduct ourselves properly as

connection is between 13:7 and 13:8, where the same Greek root *(opheil)*
appears. In 13:7 the NAB translates it by "due[s]"; in 13:8 by "owe." Varia-
tions of "love one another" (13:8) occur in 12:5: "So we, though many, are
one body in Christ and individually parts of one another"; 12:10: "Love
one another with mutual affection; anticipate one another in showing
honor"; and 12:16: "Have the same regard for one another." Further, Paul
introduced the thirty injunctions of Romans 12:9-21 with "Let love be
sincere."

In listing specific commandments of the Decalogue in Romans 13:9,
Paul follows the order of Deuteronomy 5:17-21. Leviticus 19:18 supplies
Paul with the commandment of love of neighbor. After much discussion
of the role of the law earlier in Romans 1–11, Paul sums it up. What people
tried to accomplish by living the Mosaic law Christian believers now accomplish by their faith-filled lives of loving their neighbors as themselves.

13:11-14 A passage that led to St. Augustine's conversion

This passage connects with the earlier eschatological passage of Romans
12:2: "Do not conform yourself to this age but be transformed by the renewal of your mind." Thus 13:11-14 forms an *inclusio* (see p. 83) with the
opening gambits of Paul's general exhortations. Romans 13:13-14 echoes
with earlier passages in Romans. Romans 6:13 reads: "And do not present
the parts of your bodies to sin as weapons for wickedness, but present
yourselves to God as raised from the dead to life and the parts of your
bodies to God as weapons for righteousness." See also Romans 8:12-13. In
an earlier letter Paul also used the contrast between night/darkness/evil
deeds and day/light/good deeds (1 Thess 5:4-11). Believers are to put on
the Kevlar body armor of light (13:12) and the attitude of the Lord Jesus
(13:14; see Phil 2:5-11).

In Book 8.12 of his *Confessions,* St. Augustine tells the story of hearing
a young child's sing-song of "Take and read, take and read." He went

in the day, not in orgies and drunkenness, not in promiscuity and licentiousness, not in rivalry and jealousy. ¹⁴But put on the Lord Jesus Christ, and make no provision for the desires of the flesh.

14 **To Live and Die for Christ.** ¹Welcome anyone who is weak in faith, but not for disputes over opinions. ²One person believes that one may eat anything, while the weak person eats only vegetables. ³The one who eats must not despise the one who abstains, and the one who abstains must not pass judgment on the one who eats; for God has welcomed him. ⁴Who are you to pass judgment on someone else's servant? Before his own master he stands or falls. And he will be upheld, for the Lord is able to make him stand. ⁵[For] one person considers one day more important than another, while another person considers all days alike.

---

back to the place where he had put Paul's text. He writes: "I snatched it up, opened it and in silence read the passage upon which my eyes first fell." The passage was Romans 13:13-14. St. Augustine continues: "I had no wish to read further, and no need. For in that instant, with the very ending of the sentence, it was as though a light of utter confidence shone in all my heart, and all the darkness of uncertainty vanished away" (F. J. Sheed translation). Augustine was on the threshold of casting off the desires of the flesh and giving himself over to the fruit of the Spirit.

14:1–15:13 Principles that govern conduct with regard to indifferent matters

Scholars are divided on the question of whether in Romans 14:1–15:13 Paul is addressing a concrete situation in the Roman house churches. I, for one, do not think so. Nor do I think that Paul is specifically addressing a situation where "the weak" are Jewish Christians and "the strong" are Gentile Christians. After making two methodological points, I treat the principles that Paul enunciates in this section.

A number of my readers may have already perused my commentary on Galatians in this booklet. In that letter it was fairly clear that Paul was engaged with teachers/influencers who were championing circumcision and observance of the Mosaic law. See, for example, Galatians 6:15: "For neither does circumcision mean anything, nor does uncircumcision, but only a new creation." In 1 Corinthians 8:7 the situation is clear and deals with meat sacrificed to idols: "But not all have this knowledge. There are some who have been so used to idolatry up until now that, when they eat meat sacrificed to idols, their conscience, which is *weak*, is defiled" (emphasis added).

However, when we take a close look at Romans 14:1–15:13, it is very difficult to ascertain what was going on. Eating and drinking (14:2, 21),

Let everyone be fully persuaded in his own mind. [6]Whoever observes the day, observes it for the Lord. Also whoever eats, eats for the Lord, since he gives thanks to God; while whoever abstains, abstains for the Lord and gives thanks to God. [7]None of us lives for oneself, and no one dies for oneself. [8]For if we live, we live for the Lord, and if we die, we die for the Lord; so then, whether we live or die, we are the Lord's. [9]For this is why Christ died and came to life, that he might be Lord of both the dead and the living. [10]Why then do you judge your brother? Or you, why do you look down on your brother? For we shall all stand before the judgment seat of God; [11]for it is written:

> "As I live, says the Lord, every
> knee shall bend before me,
> and every tongue shall give
> praise to God."

[12]So [then] each of us shall give an account of himself [to God].

Consideration for the Weak Conscience. [13]Then let us no longer judge one another, but rather resolve never to put a stumbling block or hindrance in the way of a brother. [14]I know and am convinced in the Lord Jesus that nothing is unclean in itself; still, it is unclean for someone who thinks it unclean. [15]If your brother is being hurt by what you eat, your conduct is no longer in accord with love. Do not because of your food destroy him for whom Christ died. [16]So do not let your good be reviled. [17]For the kingdom of God is not a matter of food and drink, but of righteousness, peace, and joy in the holy Spirit; [18]whoever serves Christ in this way is pleasing to God and approved by others. [19]Let us then pursue what leads to peace and to building up one another. [20]For the sake of food, do not destroy the work of God. Everything is indeed clean, but it is wrong for anyone to become a stumbling block by eating; [21]it is good not to eat meat or drink wine or do anything that causes your brother to stumble. [22]Keep the faith [that] you have to yourself in the presence of God; blessed is the one who does not condemn himself for what he approves. [23]But whoever has doubts is condemned if he eats, because this is not from faith; for whatever is not from faith is sin.

---

special days (14:5-6), and clean and unclean food (14:14) are vague and insufficient evidence on which to depict a battle over indifferent matters that was actually raging in or among the Roman house churches.

Moreover, I challenge my readers to find multiple references to "the weak" and "the strong" and to their positions in this passage. Romans 14:1 and 15:1 are the only two verses that refer to "the weak," while Romans 15:1 is the only verse that addresses "the strong." In our quest for finding or making order out of what Paul says, we are the ones who create the camp of "the weak" and the camp of "the strong."

As J. Paul Sampley has shown, this is indeed Paul's goal in writing so obliquely rather than directly, as he did in Galatians and 1 Corinthians.

15 **Patience and Self-Denial.** [1]We who are strong ought to put up with the failings of the weak and not to please ourselves; [2]let each of us please our neighbor for the good, for building up. [3]For Christ did not please himself; but, as it is written, "The insults of those who insult you fall upon me." [4]For whatever was written previously was written for our instruction, that by endurance and by the encouragement of the scriptures we might have hope. [5]May the God of endurance and encouragement grant you to think in harmony with one another, in keeping with Christ Jesus, [6]that with one accord you may with one voice glorify the God and Father of our Lord Jesus Christ.

God's Fidelity and Mercy. [7]Welcome one another, then, as Christ welcomed you, for the glory of God. [8]For I say that Christ became a minister of the circumcised to show God's truthfulness, to confirm the promises to the patriarchs, [9]but so that the Gentiles might glorify God for his mercy. As it is written:

> "Therefore, I will praise you among the Gentiles
>   and sing praises to your name."

[10]And again it says:

> "Rejoice, O Gentiles, with his people."

[11]And again:

> "Praise the Lord, all you Gentiles,
>   and let all the peoples praise him."

[12]And again Isaiah says:

Sampley writes: "Direct speech is argumentative and confrontational while figured speech is allusive and evocative; direct speech needs proofs, while figured speech invites the hearer to establish its veracity by self-application." I might add that Paul's two diatribal questions in 14:4, 10 help him get his listeners to apply his teaching to themselves.

If this lengthy passage doesn't deal with specific questions in the Roman house churches, then what's it all about? It's about the principles to be applied in those multiple situations that involve indifferent matters, that is, not questions of faith and morals, but which nonetheless can create ugly stains on the fabric of community life. Paul has arrived at these principles from previous experiences with communities, especially in Corinth. N. T. Wright's comment about 14:1–15:13 is helpful: "This is what justification by faith looks like when it sits down at table in Christian fellowship."

I give a few of the principles that course through this section and invite my readers to discover others as they explore Paul's interchange of the personal pronouns "you" and "we" and engage in their own self-application of Paul's teaching. "We shall all stand before the judgment seat of God" (14:10). "Nothing is unclean in itself" (14:14). "The kingdom

"The root of Jesse shall come,
    raised up to rule the Gentiles;
in him shall the Gentiles hope."

[13]May the God of hope fill you with all joy and peace in believing, so that you may abound in hope by the power of the holy Spirit.

VII. Conclusion

Apostle to the Gentiles. [14]I myself am convinced about you, my brothers, that you yourselves are full of goodness, filled with all knowledge, and able to admonish one another. [15]But I have written to you rather boldly in some respects to remind you, because of the grace given me by God [16]to be a minister of Christ Jesus to the Gentiles in performing the priestly service of the gospel of God, so that the offering up of the Gentiles may be acceptable, sanctified by the holy Spirit. [17]In Christ Jesus, then, I have reason to boast in what pertains to God. [18]For I will not dare to speak of anything except what Christ has accomplished through me to lead the Gentiles to obedience by word and deed, [19]by the power of signs and wonders, by the power of the Spirit [of God], so that from Jerusalem all the way around to Illyricum I have finished preaching the gospel of Christ. [20]Thus I aspire to proclaim the gospel not where Christ has already been named, so that I do not build on another's foundation, [21]but as it is written:

---

of God is not a matter of food and drink, but of righteousness, peace, and joy in the holy Spirit" (14:17). Paul appeals not only to principles but also to the example of Jesus Christ: "For Christ did not please himself" (15:3); "Welcome one another, then, as Christ welcomed you" (15:7). Finally, in 15:9-12 he appeals to all of Sacred Writ—the Law, the Prophets, and the Writings —to show the universality of God's welcome.

During the course of my work, I have traveled to different cultures and experienced firsthand the struggle involved in realizing that what I thought was "universal law" was an indifferent matter. St. Peter's in Rome doesn't have kneelers, yet I thought that such a practice was de rigueur. I was pleasantly surprised when I was served pea soup with ham in a German friary on a day of abstinence: "Ach, what is pea soup without ham?"

CONCLUSION

Romans 15:14–16:27

15:14-24 Paul needs the assistance of the Roman believers in spreading his gospel to Spain

I make three observations. As Paul concludes his rich letter to the Romans, he repeats three times that his gospel is for the Gentiles (15:16, 18). It is the gospel he has been preaching throughout this very letter.

"Those who have never been told
of him shall see,
and those who have never heard
of him shall understand."

Paul's Plans; Need for Prayers.
²²That is why I have so often been prevented from coming to you. ²³But now, since I no longer have any opportunity in these regions and since I have desired to come to you for many years, ²⁴I hope to see you in passing as I go to Spain and to be sent on my way there by you, after I have enjoyed being with you for a time. ²⁵Now, however, I am going to Jerusalem to minister to the holy ones. ²⁶For Macedonia and Achaia have decided to make some contribution for the poor among the holy ones in Jerusalem; ²⁷they decided to do it, and in fact they are indebted to them, for if the Gentiles have come to share in their spiritual blessings, they ought also to serve them in material blessings. ²⁸So when I have completed this and safely handed over this contribution to them, I shall set out by way of you to Spain; ²⁹and I know that in coming to you I shall come in the fullness of Christ's blessing.

³⁰I urge you, [brothers,] by our Lord Jesus Christ and by the love of the Spirit, to join me in the struggle by your

---

Second, Paul's description of having preached the gospel of Christ "from Jerusalem all the way around to Illyricum" (15:19) should be taken in a global sense, for Paul has not preached to every individual or in every town.

Finally, 15:24 should not be read as if Paul were alerting the Roman house churches that he planned to visit them during a whistle stop. The Greek behind "to be sent on my way" really means to supply food, money, companions, means of travel, and such. The Roman believers could not make all these arrangements overnight. Also, according to Joseph A. Fitzmyer, "there is thus far no evidence of Jewish habitation in Spain prior to the third century A.D." So Paul could not follow a procedure of preaching first in a Jewish synagogue. Moreover, as Robert Jewett surmises, Paul had to have the Scriptures translated "into the Celt-Iberian dialects still employed by most of the population in Spain." The nice things that Paul says about the Roman believers in 15:14, 22-24 (technically: *captatio benevolentiae*) are in service of winning them over to the task of preaching his gospel.

15:25-33 Paul's anxiety about his reception in Jerusalem

In Romans 12:8 Paul mentions the gift of generosity: "if one contributes, in generosity." Romans 12:13 exhorts: "Contribute to the needs of the holy ones." Paul is taking the collection he gathered from Gentile Christians to fulfill the pledge he made in Galatians 2:10 to help the poor

prayers to God on my behalf, [31]that I may be delivered from the disobedient in Judea, and that my ministry for Jerusalem may be acceptable to the holy ones, [32]so that I may come to you with joy by the will of God and be refreshed together with you. [33]The God of peace be with all of you. Amen.

16 **Phoebe Commended.** [1]I commend to you Phoebe our sister, who is [also] a minister of the church at Cenchreae, [2]that you may receive her in the Lord in a manner worthy of the holy ones, and help her in whatever she may need from you, for she has been a benefactor to many and to me as well.

Paul's Greetings. [3]Greet Prisca and Aquila, my co-workers in Christ Jesus, [4]who risked their necks for my life, to whom not only I am grateful but also all the churches of the Gentiles; [5]greet also the church at their house. Greet my beloved Epaenetus, who was the first-fruits in Asia for Christ. [6]Greet Mary, who has worked hard for you. [7]Greet Andronicus and Junia, my relatives and my fellow prisoners; they are prominent among the apostles and they were in Christ before me. [8]Greet Ampliatus, my beloved in the Lord. [9]Greet Urbanus, our co-worker in Christ, and my beloved Stachys. [10]Greet Apelles, who is

among the Jerusalem Christians. This money, however, is not just alms. It is a symbol of the unity of the churches: The Gentile Christians "decided to do it, and in fact they are indebted to them, for if the Gentiles have come to share in their spiritual blessings, they ought also to serve them in material blessings" (15:27).

Paul's words in 15:30-31 reveal the apprehension he has about his upcoming journey to and meeting in Jerusalem: "Join me in the struggle by your prayers to God on my behalf, that I may be delivered from the disobedient in Judea." Jews may well consider Paul, a former zealot, to be a turncoat. Jewish Christians, who are zealous for the Mosaic law, may view Paul's law-free gospel for the Gentiles as repugnant. Would the Jerusalem Christians actually reject the collection and its symbolism?

16:1-16 Five house churches and leadership roles for women

To some, Romans 16:1-16 may appear to be as inspiring as reading a church directory. To others it has become a window into Romans and the early church. Behind 16:5, 10, 11, 14, 15 there is evidence of at least five house churches in Rome, or more probably tenement house churches. See, for example, 16:5: "Greet also the church at their house," that is, the house of Prisca and Aquila.

There are eight women mentioned as active in promoting the gospel: Phoebe, Prisca, Mary, Junia, Tryphaena, Tryphosa, Persis, and Rufus's mother. I single out Phoebe and Junia for further comment. Phoebe is a

approved in Christ. Greet those who belong to the family of Aristobulus. [11]Greet my relative Herodion. Greet those in the Lord who belong to the family of Narcissus. [12]Greet those workers in the Lord, Tryphaena and Tryphosa. Greet the beloved Persis, who has worked hard in the Lord. [13]Greet Rufus, chosen in the Lord, and his mother and mine. [14]Greet Asyncritus, Phlegon, Hermes, Patrobas, Hermas, and the brothers who are with them. [15]Greet Philologus, Julia, Nereus and his sister, and Olympas, and all the holy ones who are with them. [16]Greet one another with a holy kiss. All the churches of Christ greet you.

---

wealthy woman who is a *diakonos* and *prostatis* (16:1-2). The first term may be translated as "minister" and indicates a position of responsibility in the church. Archbishop Rabanus Maurus (d. 856) commented: "This passage teaches by apostolic authority that women are also constituted in the ministry of the church" (PL 111:1605D). The second term may be translated as "benefactor," if one understands that this term indicates a person of enormous prestige and influence.

It is highly likely that Phoebe not only carried Paul's letter to the Romans to the house churches but also read it to them. You see, Phoebe was likely among the five percent of the population who could read. Further, in reading Romans, she surely had to know what it was about. Ancient letters (and manuscripts) did not have spacing, chapters and verses, and subheadings. I give a simple example. Suppose I put a recent headline in capital letters without spacing: FLORIDAKEYDEERREBOUNDS. Without too much effort you read: Florida key deer rebounds. But is "key" an adjective meaning "principal"? Does "key" refer to the Florida Keys? Is "key deer" a technical name for a special species of deer? The reader would have to know answers to these questions in order to read this simple sentence out loud meaningfully. Just think of the skill Phoebe must have if she is to navigate successfully through all the elements of scholastic diatribe that Paul used in composing his letter!

I make three points about Junia (16:7). First, she is a woman. St. John Chrysostom (d. 407), who was proficient in Greek and was a misogynist, commented: "To be an apostle is something great. But to be outstanding among the apostles, just think of what a wondrous song of praise that is. . . . Truly, how great the wisdom of this woman must have been that she was even deemed worthy of the title of apostle." Second, the fathers of the church and Greek grammar indicate that Junia is an apostle and outstanding among the apostles and not merely held in high regard by male apostles.

Against Factions. ¹⁷I urge you, brothers, to watch out for those who create dissensions and obstacles, in opposition to the teaching that you learned; avoid them. ¹⁸For such people do not serve our Lord Christ but their own appetites, and by fair and flattering speech they deceive the hearts of the innocent. ¹⁹For while your obedience is known to all, so that I rejoice over you, I want you to be wise as to what is good, and simple as to what is evil; ²⁰then the God of peace will quickly crush Satan under your feet. The grace of our Lord Jesus be with you.

Greetings from Corinth. ²¹Timothy, my co-worker, greets you; so do Lucius and Jason and Sosipater, my relatives. ²²I, Tertius, the writer of this letter, greet you in the Lord. ²³Gaius, who is host to

Third, Junia was not an apostle of a church, for nowhere in 16:7 does Paul refer to her as such. Contrast 2 Corinthians 8:23 and Philippians 2:25. I am of the opinion that Junia is an apostle in the same sense as Paul, who had seen the risen Lord (1 Cor 9:1) but was not one of the Twelve. She may have been among the five hundred who saw the risen Lord (1 Cor 15:6).

16:17-27 Final goodbye with warning and doxology

There are three strange elements in Romans 16. In the previous passage we encountered the first one. Nowhere else in his letters does Paul extend greetings to twenty-four people. He desperately wants to establish a home base among the Roman Christians for his evangelical mission to Spain.

In 16:17-20 we run into the second extraordinary element in the farewell section of a Pauline letter. Paul now warns the Romans of people who "do not serve our Lord Christ but their own appetites" (16:18). One is reminded of Philippians 3:19, where Paul warns of false teachers, whose "God is their stomach."

Words we hear or speak during a farewell provide a contemporary analogy to Paul's seemingly unmotivated warning in these verses. Sometimes farewell words do not seem motivated by the event. After the magnificently glorious celebrations that surrounded my First Mass in my parish church, I was leaving home. My father kissed me and said, "Don't forget where you've come from." To this day I remember and abide by this unmotivated farewell reminder not to overly honor myself and thereby dishonor my parents. In this warning Paul is indeed speaking "rather boldly" (15:15).

Paul ends Galatians with: "The grace of our Lord Jesus Christ be with your spirit, brothers. Amen" (6:18). He concludes his other letters in a

me and to the whole church, greets you. Erastus, the city treasurer, and our brother Quartus greet you.[24]

◄ **Doxology.** [[25]Now to him who can strengthen you, according to my gospel and the proclamation of Jesus Christ, according to the revelation of the mys-

◄ tery kept secret for long ages [26]but now manifested through the prophetic writings and, according to the command of the eternal God, made known to all nations to bring about the obedience of faith, [27]to the only wise God, through Jesus Christ be glory forever and ever. Amen.]

---

similar fashion. But once again, Romans is strange. Paul finishes with a doxology. It is fitting that Paul concludes by praising and honoring God, for God has been the theme of this very long letter. It is fitting that at the conclusion of a letter whose main purpose is to reveal God's plan for the Gentiles Paul praises God for revealing this very plan. I. Howard Marshall rightly contends that doxologies also have a hortatory purpose. Romans 16:25 asks for strengthening and perseverance and repeats some of the themes of Romans 8:25-27.

In my final comment I persevere to the end with my reading program for Romans and invite my readers to check the pronouns of this doxology: "you" and "I." Paul has the Romans ("you") at heart. At the same time, this is his doxology. He is the one who is praising and honoring God, revealing his *ethos,* showing his true colors.

BIBLIOGRAPHY

THE LETTER TO THE GALATIANS

Hans Dieter Betz, *Galatians.* Hermeneia. Philadelphia: Fortress, 1979.

James D. G. Dunn, *The Epistle to the Galatians.* Black's New Testament Commentary. Peabody, MA: Hendrickson, 1993.

G. Walter Hansen, *Galatians.* The IVP New Testament Commentary Series. Downers Grove, IL: InterVarsity Press, 1994.

R.P.C. Hanson, *Allegory and Event.* Louisville: Westminster John Knox Press, 2002.

Richard N. Longenecker, *Galatians.* Word Bible Commentary 41. Dallas: Word Books, 1990.

George Lyons, *Pauline Autobiography: Toward a New Understanding.* Atlanta: Scholars Press, 1985.

J. Louis Martyn, *Galatians.* Anchor Bible 33A. New York: Doubleday, 1998.

Mark D. Nanos, *The Irony of Galatians: Paul's Letter in First-Century Context.* Minneapolis: Fortress, 2002.

Sam K. Williams, *Galatians.* Abingdon New Testament Commentaries. Nashville: Abingdon, 1997.

THE LETTER TO THE ROMANS

James W. Aageson, "Scripture and Structure in the Development of the Argument in Romans 9–11," *Catholic Biblical Quarterly* 48 (1986) 265–289.

Frederick W. Danker, *Benefactor: An Epigraphic Study of a Graeco-Roman and New Testament Semantic Field.* St. Louis: Clayton Publishing Co., 1982.

James D. G. Dunn, *Romans 1–8, 9–16.* Word Biblical Commentary 38AB. Dallas: Word Books, 1988.

Philip F. Esler, *Conflict and Identity in Romans: The Social Setting of Paul's Letter.* Minneapolis: Fortress, 2003.

Joseph A. Fitzmyer, *Romans.* Anchor Bible 33. New York: Doubleday, 1993.

A Greek-English Lexicon of the New Testament and other Early Christian Literature. Third edition (BDAG). Revised and edited by Frederick W. Danker. Chicago: University of Chicago Press, 2000.

Bibliography

Robert Jewett, "Romans," in *The Cambridge Companion to St. Paul.* Edited by James D. G. Dunn. Cambridge: Cambridge University Press, 2003, pp. 91–104.

Luke Timothy Johnson, *Reading Romans: A Literary and Theological Commentary.* Macon, GA: Smyth & Helwys, 2001.

"Joseph and Aseneth," A new translation and introduction by C. Burchard in *The Old Testament Pseudepigrapha II.* Edited by James H. Charlesworth. Garden City, NY: Doubleday, 1985, pp. 177–247.

Ernst Käsemann, "'The Righteousness of God' in Paul," in *New Testament Questions of Today.* Philadelphia: Fortress, 1969, pp. 168–182.

Leander E. Keck, "*Pathos* in Romans? Mostly Preliminary Remarks," in *Paul and Pathos.* Edited by Thomas H. Olbricht and Jerry L. Sumney. Atlanta: Society of Biblical Literature, 2001, pp. 71–96.

I. Howard Marshall, "Romans 16:25-27—An Apt Conclusion," in *Romans and the People of God: Essays in Honor of Gordon D. Fee on the Occasion of His 65th Birthday.* Edited by Sven K. Soderlund and N. T. Wright. Grand Rapids: Eerdmans, 1999, pp. 170–184.

Paul and Empire: Religion and Power in Roman Imperial Society. Edited by Richard A. Horsley. Harrisburg: Trinity Press International, 1997, pp. 1–8.

J. Paul Sampley, "The Weak and the Strong: Paul's Careful and Crafty Rhetorical Strategy in Romans 14:1–15:13," in *The Social World of the First Christians: Essays in Honor of Wayne A. Meeks.* Edited by L. Michael White and O. Larry Yarbrough. Minneapolis: Fortress, 1995, pp. 40–52.

Stanley K. Stowers, "The Diatribe," in *Greco-Roman Literature and the New Testament: Selected Forms and Genres.* Edited by David E. Aune. Atlanta: Scholars Press, 1988, pp. 71–83.

———. *A Rereading of Romans: Justice, Jews, and Gentiles.* New Haven: Yale University Press, 1994.

Charles H. Talbert, *Romans.* Smyth & Helwys Bible Commentary. Macon, GA: Smyth & Helwys, 2002.

N. T. Wright, "The Letter to the Romans," in *The New Interpreter's Bible.* Volume X. Nashville: Abingdon Press, 2002, pp. 393–770.

Galatians

Introduction *(pages 5–8)*

1. Re-read Galatians and see whether you can truly see its broad outline as a "rebuke and request" letter.

2. During his years as an apostle Paul spent many a winter in a particular place because the roads and waterways were unsafe. During these winters he didn't just make tents, but also worked on his sermons. Can you really detect some of these sermons in the pre-formed materials that are some of the building blocks of Galatians?

3. Identify the cement (ethos, logic, and pathos) in Galatians and compare it to some speech you've recently heard.

4. How does one arrive at the views being advocated by "the teachers/ influencers" in Galatians? Does Galatians make better sense then and now, once you are able to see the positions against which Paul was arguing?

1:1-5 Address *(pages 9–11)*

1. Compare the address of Galatians with those of 1–2 Corinthians and note the differences.

2. How does Paul anticipate the theme of his whole letter in these first five verses?

3. Paul's use of an early confession of faith indicates his dependence upon those who have gone before him. How does this dependence harmonize with Paul's insistence a few verses later that his Gospel is independent of human beings?

1:6-10 Loyalty to the Gospel *(pages 11–12)*

1. Why does Paul write a "rebuke" letter to the Galatians? If Paul really cared for the Galatians, wouldn't he be sending them his very best?

2. Do these verses give us a first indication of the position of the "teachers/influencers"?

1:11–2:21 Paul's Defense of His Gospel and His Authority *(pages 12–17)*

1. In this section Paul argues by means of his own example. What is his example about? Why should the Galatians follow it?

2. What was all the fuss about in Antioch concerning inclusive table fellowship? Why did Paul attack Barnabas and Cephas/Peter when they withdrew from an inclusive table? How did these two church-men deviate from the truth of the gospel?

3. This passage has given rise to two stereotypes: Christianity is gospel and not law; Christians are righteous by faith and not by works. Discuss these hard-line positions in the light of Gal 5:6: "For in Christ Jesus, neither circumcision nor uncircumcision counts for anything, but faith working through love."

3:1–4:31 Faith and Liberty *(pages 17–27)*

1. Why is Paul's rebuke of the Galatians so strong in 3:1-5? Are the Galatians like some contemporary converts that are told that they have to say some special prayers or perform some special works to be saved?

2. Put into your own words the way that Paul tells the story of Abraham. Would his version of Abraham's story be convincing to the Galatians?

3. What should you do to implement Paul's vision in Gal 3:28: "There is neither slave nor free person, there is not male or female; for you are all one in Christ Jesus"?

4. What's Abraham got to do with "the elemental powers of the world"? Why does Paul keep going back to the Galatians' powerful experience of the Spirit?

5. When I am called upon to preach on Gal 4:21-31, I start with the Gal 4:25: "It stands in line with." How would you preach or teach this passage?

5:1–6:10 Exhortation to Christian Living *(pages 29–33)*

1. Is Paul's teaching about freedom too difficult for freedom-loving, individualistic Americans to accept?

2. Join me in studying Gal 5:20-21 very seriously as we try to get rid of the notion that "the works of the flesh" are restricted to sins of the flesh.

3. Are you in the camp that wants more law in religion or in the camp that wants religious authorities to allow more room for the Spirit to operate?

6:11-18 Conclusion *(pages 33–34)*

1. In what sense has all of Galatians been Paul's battle with the teachers/ influencers over the meaning of "the new creation" brought about by the Spirit?

2. What is your favorite image of Paul? Falling off his horse? Preaching? I would venture that it is rare to see an image of Paul being scourged for the Gospel. Why?

Romans

Introduction *(pages 35–41)*

1. In all honesty answer the question: Did you read Romans from beginning to end? If your answer is Yes, then I ask: Did a pronoun-rich reading of Romans work for you?

2. Why is it that Catholics have so little acquaintance with Romans? How can you change that situation?

3. Would you agree with this statement of the single purpose of Romans: Paul writes to convince the Roman Christians of his Gospel, so that they will support his mission to Spain with personnel and money?

4. Is it a gross understatement to maintain that the argument of Romans is: God is one and that God is fair?

1:1-15 Address *(pages 43–45)*

1. How close to the surface in his address to Christians living in Rome is Paul's criticism of emperor worship?

2. According to Paul in what does true worship consist?

1:16–3:20 Humanity Lost Without the Gospel *(pages 45–52)*

1. What experiences have you had of God's faithfulness to you and yours?

2. Would you agree with Paul that the key sin is idolatry?

3. Is Paul downplaying the magnificence of God's creatures, men and women, by accentuating their sinfulness and sins? Are we humans that bad?

3:21–5:21 Justification Through Faith in Christ *(pages 52–61)*

1. Which one of Paul's images of salvation speak most powerfully to you? Justification? Redemption? Expiation?

2. What lessons does Paul draw from forebear Abraham? Are these the same lessons that we should draw today?

3. Can you name the times that you have experienced God's love poured into your heart by the Holy Spirit?

4. Provide additional examples of how the evil deed or the good deed of a single individual has influenced hundreds upon hundreds of people.

6:1–8:39 Justification and the Christian Life *(pages 61–71)*

1. How helpful is the analogy of addiction in understanding the power of sin and the power of grace in the Christian life?

2. Has the insight that Paul is using "speech in character" in Rom 7:7–8:2 helped you to appreciate the role of the Law in Christian life? Does the Law provide the tools of self-mastery? How does the Spirit provide the tools for self-mastery?

3. Spell out the Spirit's role in the moaning and groaning of human and Christian life.

4. Can you hold hands with those Christians who have drawn much strength from the hymn of Rom 8:31-39? What part of this majestic hymn is your favorite?

9:1–11:36 Jews and Gentiles in God's Plan *(pages 71–80)*

1. For decades scholars have neglected Rom 9–11, even considering it extraneous to the points Paul is making in Romans. From what you have seen so far in Romans would you agree with contemporary scholars that Rom 9–11 is not only integral to the argument of all of Romans, but is the highpoint of that argument?

2. Throughout Paul's extensive use of Scripture in Rom 9–11 one point sounds loud and clear: "The gifts and call of God are irrevocable" (11:29). Is this a basis for serious Jewish-Christian dialogue?

3. In what ways can you make the doxology of Rom 11:33-36 your own?

12:1–15:13 The Duties of Christians *(pages 81–91)*

1. In what ways does Rom 12:1–15:13 draw out the practical implications of Paul's teaching in the previous eleven chapters?

2. How would you conduct a day of recollection based on Rom 12:9-21?

3. Can you name some indifferent matters that divide your current Christian community? How would you apply to these matters the principles that Paul states in Rom 14:1–15:13?

15:14–16:27 Conclusion *(pages 91–96)*

1. Does what Paul says in Rom 15:14-33 bolster your opinion of what his purpose(s) was in writing Romans?

2. In the Roman Catholic lectionary Rom 16:3-16 occurs once as a reading (Saturday of the 31st Week in Ordinary Time). That is, the lectionary makes no reference to Phoebe. Don't you think that Phoebe deserves better treatment than that?

3. We celebrate Timothy, Titus, and Barnabas, coworkers of Paul, as saints. Why don't we honor Junia, a fellow apostle with Paul, as a saint?

4. As you come to the end of your work on Romans, do you agree that deep down its theme is simple: God is one, and God is fair?

The arabic number(s) following the citation refer to the paragraph number(s) in the *Catechism of the Catholic Church*. The asterisk following a paragraph number indicates that the citation has been paraphrased.

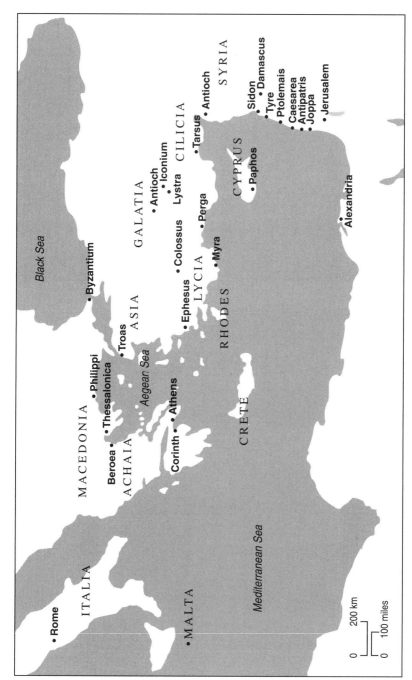

The World of Paul

107